HARRY SECOMBE'S HIGHWAY

Also by Harry Secombe from Robson Books

Fiction

Twice Brightly
Welsh Fargo

Non-fiction

Goon Abroad
The Harry Secombe Diet Book

For Children

Katy and the Nurgla

HARRY SECOMBE'S HIGHWAY

Robson Books

In association with the ITV Television series

This book is published in association with the ITV networked television series 'Highway' produced by the following ITV Companies: Anglia, Grampian, HTV, Scottish, Tyne Tees Television, Television South and Ulster.

FIRST PUBLISHED IN GREAT BRITAIN IN 1984 BY ROBSON BOOKS LTD., BOLSOVER HOUSE, 5-6 CLIPSTONE STREET, LONDON W1P 7EB. COPYRIGHT © 1984 HARRY SECOMBE

Consultant Editor: Ronnie Cass

British Library Cataloguing in Publication Data
Secombe, Harry
  Harry Secombe's Highway.
  1. Cities and towns — Great Britain
  2. Great Britain — Description and travel — 1971
  I. Title
  914.1'04858   DA632

  ISBN 0-86051-269-X

Designed: Stonecastle Graphics.
Printed in Great Britain by The Garden City Press, Letchworth
Typeset: Keyset, Maidstone, Kent.

CONTENTS

Acknowledgements   6

Preface   7

King's Lynn   11

Bath   25

Cambridge   41

Newcastle upon Tyne   57

Durham   69

Bristol   83

Swansea   98

Belfast   114

Aberdeen   129

Glasgow   143

Acknowledgements

I would like to express my warm thanks to the many people who contributed so much to the success of the 'Highway' programme — in particular Executive Producer Bill Ward and his assistant Caroline Hopkins. And a special word of thanks must go to Ronnie Cass, the Programme Associate, for his invaluable help not only on the programme itself but also in gathering together material for this book.

I would also like to thank my photographer son David, who has followed the 'Highway' trail, and many of his splendid photographs appear in the book. I am grateful, too, to the various television companies associated with the programme, the many libraries, museums, tourist boards, city councils and companies up and down the country who have been so helpful in providing additional photographs and information. A comprehensive list of photographic credits appears at the end of the book on page 160.

I would like to thank the following for allowing me to reproduce copyright material: David Higham Associates Ltd for 'Ballad of the Bread Man' by Charles Causley, from *The Collected Poems of Charles Causley* published by Macmillan, and for the extract from *A Tree With Rosy Apples* by Sid Chaplin published by Frank Graham; and William Collins and Sons and Company Ltd for 'The Nativity' by C.S. Lewis from his book, *Poems*.

Finally, grateful thanks to the many people, my guests on the 'Highway' programme, who have kindly agreed to let me include photographs of themselves.

PREFACE

When my agent, Jimmy Grafton, told me about an idea for a new television series to be called 'Highway', a kind of visual 'Down Your Way', my first reaction was one of surprise.

But Jim persisted. 'It'll be a chance to do something brand new', he said.

'Brand new? Travelling round the country again just like the old days playing in Variety, me in Scunthorpe and my laundry in Wigan? It'll be like putting the clock back I don't know how many years'.

I must admit I was pretty sceptical. Mind you, I had a reason. People can tell me that those days of the Variety Theatres were the 'good old days' until they're blue in the face, but I'm afraid I don't subscribe to the notion myself. Apart from the travelling from one unprepossessing town to another, always on a Sunday when all the railway lines were being repaired, which always put hours on the journey, there was the arrival at some dimly-lit station and the search for digs, usually in the pouring rain. I always associate looking for digs with the sound of rain gurgling down gutters and the feel of wet socks.

Then there was the challenge of facing a new audience twice-nightly every week. Every performance was like going over the top in the First World War, without the protection of our own Artillery. 'If you please 'em here, you'll please 'em anywhere' was the nightly password. And many a comic fled, sobbing, from Glasgow.

Of course I was exaggerating my reaction, I knew that, but I do enjoy having to be persuaded to do what I've already decided I should.

'Highway' was a great new concept for a programme. Each week, probably for three days, we would visit a town and film its most interesting and attractive

aspects. Then, during the course of the programme, I would meet people connected with the town — either living and working there, or famous people who had been born there: people like Wendy Craig in Durham, Patricia Brake in Bath, or Tony Britton in Bristol. Thus there would be a light-hearted, show-business element in the programme.

I was to be the link-man, and apart from talking to people, I would sing both on my own and with local choirs and orchestras.

However, the most important thing about 'Highway' was to be its 'religious' element. The programme aimed to show the 'goodness' of ordinary people doing invaluable work in the community, people who showed their faith and beliefs through their way of life and their actions: religion exemplified, in fact. Among many such people we met, three spring immediately to mind. One was Peter Griffiths, a doctor who had given up a flourishing medical practice in South Wales in order to found a hospice called Tŷ Olwyn, not far from my native Swansea. Another was Cantor Ernest Levy, who sang for us with a Jewish choir in Glasgow, and who had been in no fewer than ten concentration camps, including Belsen. The astonishing and inspiring quality about Cantor Levy was that in spite of all his suffering he was without a single trace of bitterness.

The third person I have in mind is another medical man, Dr Lloyd, who runs a premature baby unit in the hospital in Aberdeen. But it is a premature baby unit with a difference. In addition to all the superb specialised care that the unit provides, Dr Lloyd recognizes the necessity of parental love in the treatment of such premature babies. Consequently parents abound in his wards, parents who are there to love, hold and care for their tiny children.

If someone had set out to devise a programme purely to interest and appeal to me, they could not have come up with a better format than 'Highway'. It has been a joy to perform in, and a joy to recall in this book some of my many happy visits, the people I met, and the friends I made.

Harry Secombe
July, 1984

P.S. The one thing about 'Highway' which was not unmitigated delight was the schedule: for some reason the programme went from Durham to Cambridge to King's Lynn to Newcastle to Bristol to Belfast to Bath to Aberdeen to Swansea — to Glasgow. In that respect at least it was like 'the good old days' in Variety!

ING'S LYNN

You'll enjoy King's Lynn, they told me. It's small, it's relaxed, and it's peaceful. They could have fooled me! I arrived on a Tuesday morning, and I was staying at the Duke's Head Hotel.

Those of you who know King's Lynn will be ahead of me. The Duke's Head is situated in a lovely, spacious square called the Tuesday Market Place, and the reason for the square's name was in evidence all around me. A market was in full swing, with stalls covering almost every inch of the very extensive square. People apparently flood in from miles around to shop there each week because the produce is excellent, and prices are very keen.

The first part of the programme was to be shot in the market and I stepped out of the hotel right into a barrage of good-humoured banter from the stallholders.

'Lost a lot of weight, Harry boy.'

'Where's old Spike Milligan, then?'

'Sing us a song, mate.'

And other, slightly less complimentary remarks.

I had to walk through the crowd looking non-chalant until I arrived at a certain fruit stall, where I was to chat to the stallholder. It was essential that my progress was continuous as the camera was tracking me from the top of a van. On the first run, a little old lady stopped right in front of me and engaged me in a conversation about dieting.

'Start again,' said the director.

I started again, only this time to be halted in mid-stride by a burly man in overalls who had definite ideas about how I should sing 'Bless This House'.

'Again,' said the director, somewhat edgily.

'Bless this Second House', I said, grinning desperately.

Eventually I got through the crowd without being

Henry Bell's engraving of the Exchange which he designed. Built in 1683 for the town's merchants, in 1718 it became the Custom House, and is still used as such.

thwarted in my progress, reached the fruit stall, and engaged the stallholder in conversation. He looked blankly at me when I asked him the first rehearsed question.

'Wrong!' yelled the director.

'It's not me this time', I said to the floor manager.

'Yes it is', he said. 'This is the wrong fruit stall.'

It's not easy, filming outdoors . . .

If you are intending to visit Lynn (as the local people call it), then try and include a Tuesday in your programme — you'll be glad you did. However, if you can't do that, you can also go to a Friday market in the Tuesday Market Place. And if you miss that, there's a Saturday Market as well — though that's held in the Saturday Market Place. The Tuesday Market was founded in the twelfth century, and its square, surrounded by large Georgian buildings, is regarded as one of the most magnificent in Europe. The even older Saturday Market is held at the southern end of the High Street, by St Margaret's Church.

Situated on the south-east corner of the Wash, King's Lynn is one of the oldest seaports in England. The town developed around the Benedictine Priory and Church of St Margaret, founded about 1100 by Herbert de Losinga, the first Norman Bishop of Norwich. In fact, the town was originally called Bishop's Lynn, until its name was changed by Henry VIII. By the fourteenth century Lynn was ranked as England's third port, owing to its deep anchorage and an inland waterways system which by 1373 connected the town with no fewer than eight counties. Wealthy merchants established grand houses alongside the quays. These have been remarkably preserved, and the area between Queen Street and King Street contains some of the finest medieval domestic buildings in the country.

Gargoyles on St Nicholas' Chapel. Which one is Spike Milligan?

My first visit after the Tuesday Market Place was to St Nicholas' Chapel, which was built by Turbus, the third Bishop of Norwich, at the north end of the town to serve the expanding seafaring community. The chapel was rebuilt shortly before 1420, and sea-going folk have worshipped here for more than seven hundred years. A certain fisherman called Robinson Crusoe is buried here; legend has it that Daniel Defoe noted the

13

name and made it famous with his novel. Every year the King's Lynn Music Festival uses the Chapel because of its excellent acoustics, and I was privileged to hear Jane Mackenzie and the Britten Pears School Orchestra rehearse Mozart's 'Exultate Jubilate' there. It is a fine place in which to hear fine music performed.

In addition to its two market places, Lynn also boasts two medieval Guildhalls. The Hall of the Trinity Guild is in the Saturday Market Place, and is now the Town Hall. It is a dazzling building, with its chequer-board flint and stone façade, and its handsome Renaissance porch which bears the arms of Elizabeth I and James I. The undercroft, now known as the Regalia Rooms, houses the civic regalia, plate and charters dating back to 1204, when King John visited the town and granted its first Royal Charter, making it a free borough. This was when his baggage-train, following him across the Wash, badly miscalculated the tide and was lost. The Regalia Rooms also house the unique fourteenth-century enamelled silver gilt cup known as King John's Cup, Lynn's greatest treasure. With its

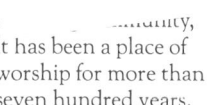

...unity, it has been a place of worship for more than seven hundred years.

The Hall of the Trinity Guild, now the Town Hall, in the Saturday Market Place. One of two medieval Guildhalls in the town, it has a most impressive chequerboard flint and stone façade and a handsome Renaissance porch built about 1580 bearing the arms of Elizabeth I and James I.

King's Lynn's greatest treasure: the unique and priceless fourteenth-century enamelled silver gilt King John's Cup which is housed in the Regalia Rooms along with the civic regalia, plate and charters dating back to 1204 when King John visited the town.

Opposite

George Chisholm showing me how to finger my umbrella.

cover, it weighs 73 ounces, and holds a pint. It's no good you working up a fine thirst, though — they won't let you drink out of it!

The other Guildhall, St George's Hall in King Street, is the largest, most ancient, and the most complete surviving example of the premises of a merchant guild in the country. It probably dates from between 1410 and 1420, and appears always to have had theatrical associations; as early as 1442 there is a record of a feast being held there which was preceded by a nativity play. Companies of Players, traditionally including Shakespeare's own, performed there, and a proper theatre was built there in 1766, after which it became in turn a granary and a wool warehouse.

Thirty-five years ago Ruth, Lady Fermoy, and Alec Penrose were responsible for saving the building in order to use it for the new Festival. Now vested in the National Trust and renamed the Fermoy Centre, it is the home of the annual King's Lynn Festival which takes place in the last week of July. Richard Rodney Bennet and Marian Montgomery, who frequently appear at the Festival with their show 'Just Friends', entertained us with two witty songs from their repertoire. Another regular at the Festival is a certain trombone player who used to deliver lines of Scottish-sounding gibberish during his appearances with his band on 'The Goon Show' — the inimitable George Chisholm. It was wonderful to meet him again and exchange reminiscences about those particular 'good old days'.

I met some more Festival performers in a less likely place than the Fermoy Centre. On the outskirts of Lynn there is a very special school for mentally handicapped children. Beautifully designed, light and airy and cheerful, the school was bright with the artwork of the pupils, and colourful pictures of clowns. On the day that I visited, the children were being entertained by Dave Swarbrick and his violin, and by Carol Crowther and her Clown Cavalcade. This remarkable lady leads a remarkable company: 'We specialize in clowning of all kinds; we're a registered charity, and we work not just in circuses and theatres but everywhere — and particularly with handicapped and disadvantaged children.'

I asked her why she did so much work with handicapped children.

'We've found — really by accident — that clowns appeal to these children immediately . . . we're their friends and we can help them through the therapy of laughter. The response we receive is wonderful. All children react in a wonderful way, but these special children react in a special way, too, because they trust us, because they love us, and you feel that you can change their lives just by coming to their school.'

Carol Crowther and her Clown Cavalcade travel around Norfolk in their pantechnicon, spreading happiness with their 'therapy of laughter'. The excitement on the faces of the children as they established an immediate rapport with the clowns, and their uninhibited delight, was a heart-warming and gladdening sight, and my admiration for the entertainers — and the teachers at the school — was redoubled when I reflected that they would be repeating their work the next day, and the next, and the days after that. How lucky we are that there are people willing to dedicate their time, love and skills to the happiness and welfare of these afflicted children.

Opposite
Here I am with Carol Crowther and her Clown Cavalcade, musician Dave Swarbrick and some local mentally-handicapped children. A remarkable lady, Carol Crowther, she travels around the country with her company — they are a registered charity — to entertain children, particularly those who are handicapped or disadvantaged in some way.

St Margaret's House, one of the town's many historic buildings. It was a merchant's house, the front of which was remodelled about 1760.

Back in the old quarter of the town, it's hard to believe that this was once just a boggy mass of marshland. The quantity of historic buildings which still survive bear witness to the skill of those early builders: St Margaret's House, large medieval warehouses going down to the river, with a fine eighteenth-century house on the street front; Priory Cottages, converted only recently from the remaining wing of de Losinga's Benedictine Priory; the Hanseatic Warehouse, erected in 1475 and used till 1751 as a depot for Hansa, the great North European merchant league; the Custom House, designed by Henry Bell, architect and sometime Mayor of Lynn, and built by Sir John Turner in 1683; the Duke's Head Hotel (named after James II when Duke of York), which has kept the original staircase and part of the gallery. It replaced the medieval Griffin Inn, and was built by Bell for Sir John Turner in 1685.

I was becoming so immersed in my discovery of this lovely old town that I'd almost forgotten I'd come here to work. The sense of history preserved was to be one of the charms of King's Lynn for me, as I discovered more about the town's unique and fascinating buildings. In contrast to the old quarter, the central part of Lynn has grown into a modern shopping centre with all the usual amenities and advantages, and yet you are never unaware that waiting round the next corner is ancient, historical King's Lynn.

Lynn is also a growing industrial area. The draining of the fens resulted in one of the richest food-producing areas in the country, and business has not been slow to capitalize on this. Canning factories now churn out the produce of local farmers. I visited one which boasts the latest techniques of mass production, and didn't know whether to be awed or terrified at the sight of one machine producing a hundred and forty cans of baked beans a minute. And that was but one machine among many.

Here I met the Reverend Derek Morton, whose job it is to work in the industrial life of the town, visiting factories, docks and workshops, and responding to the problems which confront people in an industrial society: redundancy, economic pressures, stress, fear of unemployment, and so on. As he pointed out, people

Opposite top
Priory Cottages, some of the oldest buildings in King's Lynn, are all that remains of a Benedictine Priory established about 1100 and now converted into these delightful homes.

Opposite bottom
The Hanseatic Warehouse. Erected in 1475, it was used till 1751 as a local depot for Hansa, the North European merchant league.

Detail from the Custom House: in a niche is this statue of Charles II.

spend half their waking lives at work, so there is a real reason why the Church should be concerned and involved on the shop-floor.

Part of Derek Morton's 'parish' is the seventeen acres of busy modern docks, where truckloads of exports leave for the Continent, and all the materials of modern life pass in and out of the port. Although the docks are modernized, King's Lynn is also an old harbour, and being on a river estuary it is always silting up with Fenland mud. Nature may have brought the river and its wealth to King's Lynn, but sometimes they have their work cut out to keep it there.

The local fishermen mostly fish inside the Wash, bringing home cockles, mussels, brown and pink shrimps, flounders, dabs and eels. Once upon a time they hunted whales around Greenland's shores, and indeed, until the installation of gas lighting in 1829, St Margaret's Church was lit by whale oil.

Duncan Carse, himself a seafaring man as well as being an Arctic explorer, read a dramatic account of a sea rescue, written with moving simplicity by a local

Opposite
View of the docks area. The town's importance as a trading centre has continued over the centuries to the present day.

View of Queen Street, one of several narrow streets in the old quarter of the town. Many of the buildings were merchant houses with warehouses stretching down to the river.

fisherman in a school exercise book. It was a story of adversity made even more dramatic in the telling by the fact that it was recorded in the open during a steady downpour of rain. Duncan read on, the rain beating against his face, rendering the script almost illegible, yet he never faltered, never missed a word. I found his performance quite remarkable and I began to understand something about fortitude. It made me marvel at the way men can put up with adversity without flinching and how, sometimes, that adversity brings men together to the point where they willingly risk their lives to save their fellows.

I asked Dr Alan Webster, Dean of St Paul's, who lives near Lynn, what for him made up the North Norfolk character. He summed it up as 'freedom and independence', a determination to be themselves, plan their own lives, and solve their own problems, yet in a way which involves caring for others in the community.

I thought of Carol Crowther and her clowns, and all the 'Linnets' I had met during the course of the short visit, and could not but agree.

The High Street at the turn of the century.

High Street, King's Lynn

BATH

It's amazing how one's memory can be jogged by re-visiting places one has not been to for some years, and I am constantly being reminded of odd incidents in my life as I wander up and down the country with 'Highway'.

Take Bath, for instance. When we filmed a sequence inside the Theatre Royal, I suddenly remembered playing there, back in the late 'forties, in a revue. For many reasons, too complicated to explain here, I had not had a very happy time during the run of the show, and by the time the tour had got to Bath I was getting near the end of my tether. My act had been cut to pieces, my appearances in sketches were minimal, and I was reduced to a glorified chorus boy in some of the musical numbers. And so I decided to rebel — even now I blush at my temerity. I left my act of insurrection right to the end of the show — the finale. It was a grand affair, because the principals involved had spent more money on costumes than they had on comedy material, and we all wore full evening dress — top hat, white tie and tails, and cloaks with beautiful scarlet linings.

We all made our little bows in the 'who's best' walk-down, and then lined up at the foot of a flight of tinsel-covered stairs, lifting our top hats and opening our cloaks to form a colourful setting for the leading lady's entrance in her crinoline. Usually this always brought a loud chorus of 'oohs' and 'aahs' from the audience. But not on this last night's performance. Instead there was loud laughter, much to the consternation of everybody but one on stage. Because as she reached the bottom of the stairs, my cloak opened to reveal the undying legend 'Eat at Joe's'. It cost me the price of a cloak, but, by Heavens, it was worth it.

That's one reason why Bath is one of my three favourite cities . . . (the others are Norwich and York,

Playbill for the 1805 opening performance at the Theatre Royal. A bit before my time.

with Cambridge a close fourth). You don't have to search for places to visit and explore — the beauty of Bath with its honey-coloured, stone-fronted buildings is all around you. It is the most complete and best preserved Georgian city in Britain, and its celebrated architecture draws visitors from all over the world. It was the creation of the architect John Wood, who settled in Bath in 1727. Another fine architect, Robert Adam, designed Bath's unique Pulteney Bridge, a road lined with shops across the Avon.

As the programme opened, I was riding along the magnificent sweep of the Royal Crescent (the work of Wood's son, John Wood the Younger) in a carriage drawn by two immaculately-groomed black horses. The driver and footman were in superb eighteenth-century costume, such as might have been worn in Georgian times when Bath was in its heyday, and had become a byword for elegance and fashion, with the fastidious Beau Nash bringing the elite of London and Continental society to the baths, balls and assemblies.

Opposite
The famous Theatre Royal at Bath, which has stood on this site since 1805 — in spite of my performance there!

Opening shot of the programme: I am riding along the magnificent sweep of the Royal Crescent in a carriage drawn by two immaculately groomed black horses. I was freezing in there.

The Royal Crescent provided lodgings for this privileged high society while they took the waters and enjoyed the 'season'. No. 1 Royal Crescent is a showplace now; built in 1767 for the father-in-law of John Wood the Younger, it has been beautifully restored and furnished in period style so that visitors can see exactly what it must have looked like when new.

I drove in style from the Crescent to the Circus, a marvellous circular terrace, before drawing up at the Pump Room. It looked wonderful; what the television cameras couldn't show was that it was a bitingly cold day. The sun was shining, but the wind had an edge like a knife, and sitting in the carriage while they did take after take, I gradually froze. Another thing the cameras didn't show was the regular 'plop plop' of steaming manure thudding into the roadway. I swear they must have given those horses a diet of syrup of figs and molasses the previous night. The coachman's rhubarb must be six feet high by now!

The Pump Room was built on top of the Roman precinct in the eighteenth century and has been the centre of the city's social life for the past two hundred

The Royal Crescent, begun in 1767 by John Wood the Younger, it is Bath's best known street.

and fifty years, ever since Dr William Oliver built a bath here for the treatment of gout early in the eighteenth century. Here you can drink a never-ending supply of the pure, warm mineral water that Sam Weller in *The Pickwick Papers* described as having 'a very strong flavour o' warm flat-irons'. It is thought to come from the Mendips to the south of Bath, and I was told by the curator of the Roman Museum that this very same water that wells up today probably fell as rain during the Stone Age!

The city's history goes back to AD 44 when it became an important Roman settlement, Aquae Sulis ('the waters of Sulis', a Celtic goddess). How glad the Romans must have been to find a warm place in this cold Northern island of ours, so far from the warmth of the Italian sun. Here they luxuriated in the hot springs that well up from the earth, and with their superb engineering ability built the Great Bath, eighty feet long, forty feet wide and six feet deep. It has a vaulted roof, and the hot water that runs into the bath still comes through a portion of the lead conduit laid down by a Roman plumber nearly two thousand years ago. Also, still in position in a groove in the floor is a length of lead piping that brought cold water from another source, and was used for drinking or as a cold spray.

Aquae Sulis was destroyed by the Saxons in AD 577. The baths silted up, the roof and walls collapsed, and the amazing Roman bathing establishment disappeared from view, and lay buried and preserved until the eighteenth century. In 1727 workmen digging a sewer broke through part of a very old building. They were about 16 feet down under Stall Street, and had stumbled on part of a Roman hypocaust (that's the space below the floor into which the Romans used to pipe hot air to warm the rooms). They also discovered a gilded bronze head of Minerva, the Roman goddess of healing. The subsequent excavation of the baths and all the fascinating discoveries that were made is a subject large enough for a book. The important thing is that these Roman remains are the best-preserved of any in the country.

The eighteenth-century writers Tobias Smollett and Henry Fielding both described Bath in their novels, and

the city appears in the works of Jane Austen and Charles Dickens in the nineteenth century, when it was still a fashionable resort. This is how Dickens described the Pump Room: 'Ball nights there are moments snatched from Paradise, rendered bewitching by music, beauty, elegance, fashion, etiquette and above all — the absence of tradespeople'. He wrote a great deal more about the Pump Room in *The Pickwick Papers*, where Pickwick sojourns in Bath for several months and hobnobs with the town's high society. It was amusing to dress up as Pickwick once again, and enact a light-hearted, fanciful meeting with Beau Nash Junior (played by Leslie Crowther, who lives a few miles outside Bath and is quite fanatical about his adopted city).

Dickens, by the way, got the name Pickwick from Bath, where the White Hart Hotel was owned by one Moses Pickwick. He also owned a livery stable and ran a daily service from Bath, and there is a curious story about him. It is said that he was the descendant of a foundling picked up by the side of the road by a woman who was passing through the village of Wick, near Bath. She took the baby home, looked after him, and named him Eleazer Pickwick — picked up in Wick!

Opposite
The Roman Baths. How glad the Romans must have been to find a warm place in this cold Northern island of ours!

With Leslie Crowther in our *Pickwick* costumes. He wanted to buy his — provided 'The Price was Right'!

Having tea with actress Patricia Brake in the elegant Pump Room, centre of the city's social life for over 250 years. Her reading of Charles Causley's 'Ballad of the Bread Man' proved to be one of the most popular items in the series.

I met that talented actress and local girl Patricia Brake in the Pump Room, and she read a poem by the Cornish poet Charles Causley. It proved to be one of the most popular items in the whole of the first series of 'Highway':

BALLAD OF THE BREAD MAN

Mary stood in the kitchen
  Baking a loaf of bread.
An angel flew in through the window.
  'We've a job for you,' he said.

'God in his big gold heaven,
  Sitting in his big blue chair,
Wanted a mother for his little son.
  Suddenly saw you there.'

Mary shook and trembled,
  'It isn't true what you say.'
'Don't say that,' said the angel.
  'The baby's on its way.'

It was election winter.
    They went to vote in town.
When Mary found her time had come
    The hotels let her down.

The baby was born in an annexe
    Next to the local pub.
At midnight, a delegation
    Turned up from the Farmers' Club.

They talked about an explosion
    That made a hole in the sky,
Said they'd been sent to the Lamb & Flag
    To see God come down from on high.

A few days later a bishop
    And a five-star general were seen
With the head of an African country
    In a bullet-proof limousine.

'We've come', they said, 'with tokens
    For the little boy to choose'.
Told the tale about war and peace
    In the television news.

After them came the soliders
    With rifle and bomb and gun,
Looking for enemies of the state.
    The family had packed and gone.

When they got back to the village
    The neighbours said, to a man,
'That boy will never be one of us,
    Though he does what he blessed well can'.

He went round to all the people
    A paper crown on his head.
Here is some bread from my father.
    Take, eat, he said.

Nobody seemed very hungry,
    Nobody seemed to care.
Nobody saw the god in himself
    Quietly standing there.

He finished up in the papers.
  He came to a very bad end.
He was charged with bringing the living to life.
  No man was that prisoner's friend.

There's only one kind of punishment
  To fit that kind of a crime.
They rigged a trial and shot him dead.
  They were only just in time.

They lifted the young man by the leg,
  They lifted him by the arm,
They locked him in a cathedral
  In case he came to harm.

They stored him safe as water
  Under seven rocks.
One Sunday morning he burst out
  Like a jack-in-the-box.

Through the town he went walking.
  He showed them the holes in his head.
Now do you want any loaves? he cried.
  'Not today,' they said.

A view of Bath from an 1850 edition of *The Illustrated London News*. It was described as 'a handsome city, long noted for the beauty of its buildings, which consist almost entirely of stone, and present a finer appearance than any other city in England'.

The morning that I had free I spent not at the Cheddar Gorge, not at Longleat House, nor Castle Combe (elected the prettiest village in England in 1962), nor the caves at Wookey Hole; all of them worthy of visiting and all accessible from Bath. I went to Lacock, one of the most beautiful, unspoilt villages in England, which is almost entirely made up of fifteenth and sixteenth-century houses, complete with cobbled streets and stocks. The twentieth century is not allowed to intrude; there are no television aerials, and no advertisements luridly proclaiming the superiority of soap powder X over soap powder Y. It's amazing how restful this liberation from eye-assaulting advertising is.

There are shops, of course, mainly craft shops selling beautiful individual work. Silverware is a speciality. But the pièce de résistance is Lacock Abbey,

A view of the village of Lacock. One of the most beautiful, unspoilt villages in England, it is made up almost entirely of fifteenth and sixteenth-century houses.

Lacock Abbey, the last religious house in England to be dissolved after the Reformation. Founded in 1232, it still retains its thirteenth-century cloisters, sacristy and nuns' chapter.

Opposite

Bath Abbey, founded in 1499 by Bishop Oliver King on the site of a Saxon abbey, and where in the tenth century Edgar was crowned first King of England. It is here that I was privileged to sing with the Abbey Choir and the Wessex Chamber Choir Fred Wetherley's 'The Holy City'.

which, like most of the village, is owned by the National Trust. Founded in 1232, it still retains its thirteenth-century cloisters, sacristy and nuns' chapter. It was the last religious house in England to be dissolved after the Reformation, and it was converted to a mansion by Sir William Sharington in about 1540. A keen photographer myself, I was very interested to learn that it was the home of William Henry Fox Talbot, a pioneer of photography, during the nineteenth century.

If you think you don't know Lacock, you may be wrong — film companies have long since discovered its attractions. The village is one huge, period set, and there is no expensive work to be done removing tell-tale signs of twentieth-century living, such as had to be done in Castle Combe, for instance, when the film *Doctor Doolittle* was being made. So you may have seen Lacock without ever knowing it!

By the afternoon I was back in Bath again and at work on the programme. The city has so much to be proud of, and nobody is more aware of this than the Mayor and Town Council. One of the city's projects that has involved all of Bath's inhabitants is the restoration, at the cost of millions of pounds, of the

Theatre Royal, which only three years ago was in danger of closing — and they couldn't blame me this time. It was opened before the Battle of Waterloo in 1805, and it is good to know that, thus restored, the theatre can provide entertainment for another century and a half. While I was there the stage was being got ready for the Kent Opera Company's production of *Robinson Crusoe*. I begin to wonder if Crusoe is the linking theme of this book, having come across him in King's Lynn and Bristol, too! Come to think of it, it was *Friday* second house that I performed my naughty cloak bit.

Before I left Bath I was given the opportunity to sing in Bath Abbey with the Abbey Choir and the Wessex Choir. The Abbey was founded in 1499 on the site of a Saxon abbey, where in the tenth century Edgar was crowned first King of England. Choosing a song was not difficult. Inevitably it was one written by a man from Bath, one of the best-loved sacred songs of all time: Fred Wetherley's 'The Holy City'. It was a fine way to take my leave of this beautiful city.

Pulteney Bridge, designed by Robert Adam in 1771. This unique bridge forms a road lined with shops across the River Avon.

Opposite
The Great West Door of the Abbey.

CAMBRIDGE

I left school at the age of sixteen, and ninety-five per cent of what knowledge I have today has been acquired since then. Consequently I regard higher education and scholastic achievements with some awe, and it was not without the hope of impressing my wife, Myra, that I announced, in a deliberately casual manner, 'I'm going to Cambridge.'

Myra was unimpressed.

'Oh yes?' she said, busying herself with my suit-case. 'Let's hope they teach you to pack a bit better.'

'What?' I said.

'You haven't packed any socks.'

'No — well — I was going to buy some when I got there,' I said defensively.

As usual, Myra was not fooled.

Actually I did feel a thrill of anticipation at the thought of spending some time in Cambridge. I had been there before, of course, but mainly for one night stands, with only enough time to become acquainted with some local musicians, and yet another backstage area, and I can assure you, when you've seen one back-stage area you've seen them all. It had been doubly frustrating to know that the splendours of Cambridge were all around me, and yet they might have been on the other side of the world for all the chance I would have of visiting them. Now I was to have two whole days there specifically to *visit*. Not only would I be shown around by experts, but I would have time to browse for myself.

The weather was perfect when I arrived and unpacked at the Garden Hotel (noting that a generous supply of socks was now in my suitcase). My first stop was to be King's College Chapel, one of the finest examples of fifteenth-century Perpendicular archi-tecture in Britain. I could spend forever marvelling at

King's College, founded by Henry VI in 1441, is one of the finest examples of fifteenth-century Perpendicular architecture in Britian.

View of King's Parade. Facing King's College, it is the best known street in Cambridge.

this dazzling nonpareil, standing out as it does even from the breathtakingly beautiful buildings around it. However, I will confine myself to mentioning one or two things which had most impact on me. The first was the glorious view you get of the Chapel as you approach from the river, and the sense of peace and serenity which it imparts. Second is the beautiful fan-vaulted roof, decorated with fleur-de-lis and trefoils. Another is the magnificent, intricately-carved organ screen in which are cut the initials of Henry VIII and Anne Boleyn. Finally there is Rubens' masterpiece, 'The Adoration of the Magi', which forms the altarpiece of the Chapel.

Feeling uplifted and spiritually refreshed, I made my way outside into busy King's Parade. I stepped off the pavement and was almost run down by a passing cyclist. I should have known better — bicycles are to Cambridge what rats were to Hamelin. I looked carefully before attempting to cross again, and suddenly my ears were assailed by a pleasant sound. Burrowing my way into the crowd, I soon discovered the source: two graduates who had ended up on the streets. Actually it was the Cambridge Buskers, now a well-known act. They had been students together at the University and to eke out their grant had got together to do a little busking on the side. They had proved to be very good at it, and the upshot was that the two had decided to turn professional. They play a bewildering number of instruments and produce a most appealing sound. I stood listening to them, thoroughly enjoying their music, and then chatted to them and learnt more about some of the instruments they played.

I just had time before lunch to browse in a few of the many bookshops. That is one of the reasons I so enjoy visiting Cambridge — it's full of bookshops. The town must have the fattest bookworms in the world! The Cambridge University Press is here. They are the oldest publishers of the world's best-selling book — the Bible. And there is a particular bible that the Press can

The Cambridge Buskers: Michael Copley (left) and David Ingram met while students in Cambridge. They started busking in order to eke out their grant, but became so successful that on leaving Cambridge they turned professional.

be justly proud of. It is a 1638 edition of the King James', or Authorized, version which only three presses in the country are allowed to print, partly because of their consistent accuracy. Ever since 1591, this Press has been turning out bibles and prayer books for countries all over the world. They've lost count of how many millions they've printed. Printing bibles is, in fact, a delicate operation. Special, extra thin paper has to be used to enable all those words to be bound up into one

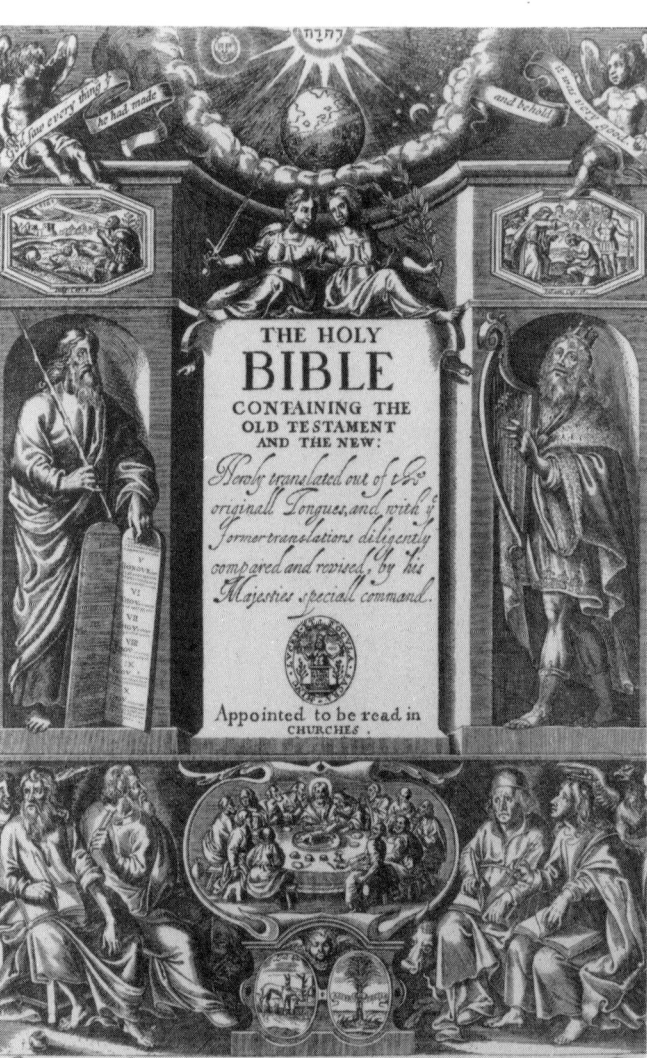

Title page from the Buck and Daniel Folio Bible of 1629 which is renowned for its textual accuracy. Thomas Buck and Robert Daniel were University Printers at Cambridge in the early seventeenth century.

normal-sized book. It calls for a high level of skill, which has been passed on through four hundred years of printing at the Cambridge University Press.

I had enough free time in the afternoon to take a punt ride down the Cam, along The Backs. The Cam, once called the Granta, is the river from which Cambridge derives its name, and The Backs are literally the backs of the Colleges lining the river. The combination of tranquil water, mellow stone, spacious, immaculately-tended lawns and graceful trees is quite magnificent. Each of the Colleges you glimpse tantalizingly through their courts and gardens has a fascinating history, and each bridge under which you pass, from the wooden Mathematical Bridge which was originally built in 1749 without nails, to the lovely fifteenth-century stone bridge of Clare College — the oldest bridge — is worthy of study.

So, how do you relax and enjoy the beauties of a trip down the Cam, and at the same time remain alert for all the points of interest any guide will insist you take notice of? Make the punt-trip twice, that's how.

Clare College Bridge. Built of stone in the fifteenth century, it is the oldest bridge in Cambridge.

The first time, just give yourself up to the splendours of the scenery; the second time go down as a tourist, guide-book in hand, ready to spot and identify landmarks.

I was in the fortunate position of knowing that I would be going down the river again the following day as part of the programme, and I continued in the punt as far as Grantchester, made famous by the First World War poet Rupert Brooke. In the garden of the Old

Opposite
View of the Mathematical Bridge which spans the River Cam. The bridge is made of wood and was originally built in 1749 without nails. Queens' College is on the right — with nails!

The Old Vicarage at Grantchester, two miles south-west of Cambridge, home of poet Rupert Brooke. It took me a couple of hours to journey down the Cam on a punt to get there — and when I arrived he wasn't in!

Vicarage where he once lived I was to have, the next day, the moving experience of hearing Sarah Jones — the courageous widow of Colonel 'H' Jones, who was killed in the Falklands War — read Brooke's poem, *The Soldier*:

If I should die, think only this of me:
    That there's some corner of a foreign field
That is for ever England. There shall be
    In that rich earth a richer dust concealed;
A dust whom England bore, shaped, made aware,
    Gave, once, her flowers to love, her ways to roam,
A body of England's, breathing English air,
    Washed by the rivers, blest by suns of home.

And think, this heart, all evil shed away
    A pulse in the eternal mind, no less
Gives somewhere back the thoughts by England given;
    Her sights and sounds; dreams happy as her day;
    And laughter, learnt of friends; and gentleness,
    In hearts at peace, under an English heaven.

The following morning I realized that already half my time in Cambridge had gone, and I had only scratched the surface of this lovely city. That was why I took the unprecedented step of being up and breakfasted by six-thirty. I wasn't needed for filming until nine-thirty, and I had decided that I would thoroughly 'do' one of the twenty-four Colleges which go to make up the University. But which one? I knew I would be visiting St John's for 'Highway', so it wouldn't be that one. Eventually I settled on Trinity.

I set off to walk through the early morning sunshine of a beautiful late summer day. I had the town almost to myself, and it was strange to think that these deserted streets would soon be teeming with bustling students. How many generations of students must have trodden these very streets, their heads full of knowledge and ideas, their hearts full of hopes and dreams?

Soon I found myself outside a very sleepy Trinity College. As I gazed up at the Great Gate with its statue of Henry VIII, I became aware of someone standing at my elbow. He introduced himself simply as Alan, and

Opposite

Sarah Jones, widow of Colonel 'H' Jones who was killed in the Falklands War, reading Brooke's poem 'The Soldier' in the garden of the Old Vicarage.

48

Trinity College, the largest college in Cambridge, with its beautiful Renaissance fountain and Edward III tower. Its magnificent Great Court is larger than any other court in Cambridge.

proceeded to take me on a superb conducted tour of the College.

Trinity, he told me, was founded by Henry VIII as one of the last acts of his life, and is the largest college in Cambridge, having absorbed two earlier colleges when it came into existence. Its magnificent Great Court is larger than any other Court in Cambridge, and its library was built by Sir Christopher Wren, who modelled it on the library of St Mark's in Venice. The College's many distinguished pupils and Fellows include Isaac Newton, Francis Bacon, Dryden, Byron (who is said to have kept a dancing bear there), Tennyson, Macaulay, Thackeray, Bulwer Lytton, and a host of scientists, among them Rutherford and Thomson.

Lord Adrian, sometime master of Trinity, once said: 'The time may come when the colleges may become almshouses for the old, and cafeterias for the young, but it will always be something to have fallen asleep to the sound of the fountain playing in Trinity Great Court.' Looking at the splendid Renaissance fountain, I had to agree.

I was amused to see evidence of Cambridge class distinction, as those few undergraduates who were awake took the long way round the outer edges of the lawns, upon which they are not allowed to set foot, while the Fellows, with the air of someone who's been given the key to the executive washroom, walk across them in deliberately casual fashion.

I admired the beautiful clock in the Edward III tower before walking through the graceful archway underneath. This tower, which was originally the gateway to one of the two colleges with which Trinity merged at its founding, was actually moved back twenty yards, stone by stone, by the Master of Trinity in 1615 in order to create the present Great Court. Once again I was riveted by the thought of so much history, so much tradition, distilled in these beautiful, serene buildings, and it took quite an effort of will to remind myself that I was in the here-and-now, and that time was flying past. Why is it that today life seems such a race against the clock? Was time always so short?

Feeling very self-righteous I returned to the Garden Hotel to join the rest of the film unit. That morning I was to go down the river again, this time in the company of Peter Atkin. There was a particular reason for my interview with Peter: that year (1983) was the centenary of The Footlights, the Cambridge Theatrical Society, which has made such an impact on the entertainment profession, especially in recent years. Many an aspiring scholar has gone to Cambridge with the genuine intention of burying his nose in the appropriate textbooks for three or four years, and emerging with a first-class honours degree, only to be seduced from his purpose and tempted into a profession quite different from that which he'd intended. Among the many who have fallen victim to the lure of The Footlights are John Cleese, Peter Cook, Graeme Garden, Eric Idle, Jonathan Miller, Griff Rhys-Jones, Clive James, Robert Buckman, Tim Brooke-Taylor, David Frost, Jonathan Routh, Richard Baker, Jimmy Edwards, Eleanor Bron, Joe Melia, John Bird, Trevor Nunn, Bill Oddie, Jo Kendall, Graham Chapman, Jack Hulbert, Julie Covington, and someone who I'm personally very glad became involved with The Footlights because he later

A 1950s Footlights production with Eleanor Bron, Peter Cook (far right) and Timothy Birdsall (far left). The Footlights, the Cambridge Theatrical Society, celebrated its centenary in 1983.

wrote the lyrics of a song that I adore singing, 'If I Ruled the World' — Leslie Bricusse.

There is, you will notice, a great preponderance of males in the list. That is because until recently women were not allowed in The Footlights. However, from all this a moral emerges: to misquote Noel Coward, 'If you don't want your son on the stage, Mrs Worthington, don't send him to Cambridge'.

I had a delightful morning floating up and down the Cam, listening to tales of The Footlights from Peter Atkin, before we adjourned for lunch. Then there was just time for a quick walk around the town before completing the programme in the afternoon. I thought I could not do better than by starting in King's Parade, dodging the bicycles like an expert slalom racer, looking at the students crammed together in tea-shops like the Copper Kettle, exchanging gossip and ideas, resolving the world's problems over their tea-cups, arguing politics and philosophy, forging lifelong bonds of friendship. From the Parade I turned into St Mary's Street, then up Market Hill, before walking past the famous Arts Theatre. I strolled as far as Emmanuel College, and then on to the immortal Parker's Piece, the University cricket ground, with its well-tempered wicket that has provided many a county cricketer with a useful start to the season in a match against the University team.

I arrived back at the hotel to find that a search party was about to set out to look for me, and the film unit proceeded to St John's College.

Parker's Piece, the University cricket ground. (Not the lady in the foreground!)

St John's was founded in 1511 in memory of Lady Margaret Beaufort, the mother of Henry VII, on the site of a hospital. The second largest college in Cambridge, it lies on both sides of the Cam, its bridge being the Bridge of Sighs, whose five unglazed windows give it the look of a cloister. The College's Great Gateway is the finest in Cambridge, with its magnificent display of heraldic devices which include the Tudor Rose, the Beaufort Portcullis, and Lady Margaret's insignia of daisies, or marguerites, together with the coats of arms of England and France.

I was to talk there to one of St John's most famous ex-pupils, former Archbishop of Canterbury, Lord Coggan. As I waited for him, I chatted to the college porter who, like all Cambridge college porters, displayed a fanatical regard for his own college. Possibly to make me feel at home, he told me that their Chemistry professor, who was Welsh, was in charge of the College's rugby team.

'Send him down to the National Stadium', I told him prophetically. 'We might need him.'

Opposite
St John's College was founded in 1511 and is the second largest college in Cambridge. Its boat club, founded in 1825, is the oldest in Cambridge and the challenge by one of its members to Oxford was the forerunner of the now famous Boat Race.

With Lord Coggan, the former Archbishop of Canterbury. A man of unexpected warmth and wit, it was he who impressed upon me the extraordinary hold that Cambridge has on people.

Talking to Lord Coggan made me realize more than ever the extraordinary lifelong hold — the 'indelible impression' — that Cambridge has on people. It is not necessarily what they learn there that is of the greatest importance, but rather the overwhelming effect of the Cambridge experience. Using a most effective analogy, Lord Coggan likened Cambridge and its influence on the wider world to the dropping of a pebble in a pool: the ripples spread ever outward.

It was the end of an unforgettable two days for me, and I was certain that the ripples from Cambridge, and the memory of its timeless beauty, would stay with me for many a long day. William Wordsworth was a St John's man, albeit an apparently undistinguished scholar during his time there, and I cannot do better than close this chapter with the following lines from *The Prelude*, which so aptly sum up my own feelings about Cambridge:

> *I could not print*
> *Ground where the grass had yielded to the steps*
> *Of generations of illustrious men,*
> *Unmoved. I could not always lightly pass*
> *Through the same gateways, sleep where they had*
> *slept,*
> *Wake where they had waked, range that inclosure*
> *old,*
> *That garden of great intellects, undisturbed.*
> *Place also by the side of this dark sense*
> *Of noble feeling, that those spiritual men,*
> *Even the great Newton's own ethereal self,*
> *Seemed humbled in these precincts thence to be*
> *The more endeared. Their several memories here*
> *(Even like their persons in their portraits clothed*
> *With the accustomed garb of daily life)*
> *Put on a lowly and touching grace*
> *Of more distinct humanity, that left*
> *All genuine admiration unimpaired.*

NEWCASTLE UPON TYNE

It was appropriate that as 'Highway' comes under the administration of Tyne Tees Television, Newcastle upon Tyne should be the launching pad for the programme. This was the testing time for me and for my team: Bill Ward, Executive Producer and friend of many years' standing, and Ronnie Cass, a fellow Welshman and boon companion, whose official designation of Programme Associate covers a multitude of tasks — music arranger, personal accompanist, writer of links, among others. He is also the possessor of the slyest humour west of the Brecon Beacons — or east, for that matter. We formed the central unit of 'Highway', moving into the different regional TV areas, working with new directors and crews in each area.

I remembered Newcastle from my days as a touring Variety performer, and indeed most of my previous knowledge of the towns and cities we visited on 'Highway' was gleaned from my weekly 'stands' in the respective Music Halls. My recollections of Newcastle were of surprisingly sophisticated audiences — surprising, because only a few miles away at the Sunderland Empire many a famous comedian had been broken by the steely silence which greeted his performance. So I had high hopes for Newcastle being a good place to begin our new venture, and the three of us set off from Heathrow in optimistic spirits.

The first place I visited was the Tyne Bridge (one of the six bridges within the space of a single mile), formerly known as the George V Bridge, where I met Colin Douglas, well known for his role in the television series, 'A Family at War', and an expert on Newcastle's bridges. He told me that the similarity I had remarked between the single span Tyne Bridge and the Sydney Harbour Bridge was not surprising: 'This was the prototype for the Sydney Bridge', he told me, with more than

The Quayside Market, held under the Tyne and High Level Bridges, attracts over 20,000 people every Sunday. It has been in existence for more than eight hundred years.

a touch of civic pride. 'I was on this bridge the day it was opened by King George V, the 10th of October, 1928.'

'What time?' I asked mischievously.

'11.35,' he replied without blinking.

Although it was a Sunday morning the bridge was tremendously busy. People were crossing it very purposefully, clearly in a hurry to get somewhere important. They were on their way to the Quayside Market, Colin told me. My ears pricked up at that; there's nothing I like better than a market. As we went I became aware for the first time of something that was to become more apparent as I travelled round the country. Simply put, it is this: that there is nothing in a city that does not belong to, or is not descended from, the past, which is not equally becoming a part of the future.

The Quayside Market was a perfect example of what I mean. This outdoor market which runs beneath the Tyne and High Level Bridges in a former centre of water traffic was sited so that traders could take advantage of shoregoing sailors with money to spend. In the old days the market also offered the services of quack doctors and dentists, and travelling musicians would sell their ballads. The earliest 'commercials' were sung here by William Purvis, known as Blind Willy, who was born in 1762, and who used to put traders' names into his songs. We heard a local group called the High Level Ranters perform a market song such as Blind Willy might have sung, called 'Buy Broom Buzzems'.

If you want a sweetie for to clag your jaw,
I'll fill you up a quarter, mebbe even more.

Buy broom buzzems, buy them when they're new,
Fine heather bred 'uns, better never grew.

Bullets and gobstoppers, treacle toffee too,
Any kind of sweetie, for to suck and chew.

If you want a puppy or a kitten too,
Haway up, me hinnies, I've the pet for you.

Rabbits for the young 'uns, a budgie for your wife,
Tortoises and gerbils, I've selled them all me life.

Have yourself a shuggy on me roundabout,
Listen to the bairnies, hear them bawl and shout.

Fetch the young 'uns missus, come and have a treat,
Off we go again, man, it's hard to beat.

Jeans and fancy trousers, best of all you'll see,
You'll never beat me prices, buy it from the Quay!

Shirts and bonnie jackets, last you all your life,
If it's too big for you, how about the wife?

Buy broom buzzems, buy them when they're new,
Fine heather bred 'uns, better never grew.

The market has been going for over eight hundred years, and every Sunday between twenty and twenty-five thousand people flock there in search of bargains, pleasure and entertainment.

Opposite
The Castle keep, built in 1172-77. The hall occupies the whole of the interior and is reached by an external staircase up which Richard Clayderman's piano was hauled. Just imagine!

A view of Hadrian's Wall, the great Roman frontier. A bridge known as *Pons Aelius* was built across the Tyne in about 122 AD and formed part of Hadrian's Wall.

I returned to my hotel in Grey Street, The Turk's Head, one of the few hotels which ever housed all the Goons at the same time. Years ago we recorded a special 'Goon Show' called 'The Starlings', which for some reason that escapes me now was done from the Newcastle Studios. It was the only show we ever did outside London and, incidentally, was the only one performed without an audience. It so happened that Michael Bentine was playing the Empire that week and we all decided to stay together at The Turk's Head. I don't think the management ever got over it.

There was one incident during the making of 'Highway' which could have come straight out of a Goon Show script. The principal guest artist was Richard Clayderman, the highly-esteemed pianist, and someone decided it would be a great idea to have him playing his grand piano in the Castle. The story of how that instrument was eventually hauled up the steps and into position will no doubt be told elsewhere some day. Suffice it to say it was another 'first' for Newcastle.

As I've already mentioned, you cannot separate a city's present from its past, and Newcastle's roots go back to Roman times, when the bridge known as *Pons Aelius* was built across the Tyne in about 122 AD. Guarded by a fort, it formed part of Hadrian's Wall, the Roman frontier system of defence.

The Normans also realized the strategic importance of the site, with its proximity to Scotland, its control of the river crossing, and its possibilities as a port. In 1080 Robert Curthose, son of William the Conqueror, built a wooden fort, the 'New Castle', there, and a town grew up in its shadow which by 1400 had been made a county, with its own Sheriff. Henry II built another castle on the site of the original in 1172 at the exorbitant cost of £911 10s 9d. The massive 82-foot high keep, and the elegant lantern-tower of the mainly medieval St Nicholas Cathedral, can be seen from whichever bridge the visitor chooses to cross from the south. Steep flights of narrow steps between seventeenth-century warehouses lead down from the castle enclosure to the quayside.

One cannot mention Newcastle without thinking of coal, which by the early seventeenth century had succeeded wool as the most important trading commodity, and which formed the basis of Newcastle's commercial prosperity. In the boom years of the

Newcastle is of course famous for its coal industry. A Thomas Hair engraving of the 1830s shows the coal drops at Wallsend; it was at this time that coal succeeded wool as the most important trading commodity and was to form the basis of Newcastle's commercial prosperity.

The lovely park of Jesmond Dene to the north-east of the city. Newcastle has an amazing 1,400 acres of open spaces.

Victorian era, city planners took the opportunity to redevelop the city centre, and builder Richard Grainger, architect John Dobson and town clerk John Clayton were responsible for creating a fine new centre with the gracefully proportioned, broad thoroughfares of Grainger Street and Grey Street, still preserved today and once described as 'one of the most imposing façades in Europe'.

The city has 1,400 acres of open spaces, including Town Moor to the north-west and the lovely park of Jesmond Dene to the north-east, and the glorious Northumberland National Park, with its unspoilt coast and countryside, is on the doorstep.

One of Newcastle's most interesting buildings is Blackfriars, one of the most complete Dominican Friaries surviving in Britain. Founded in the thirteenth century, it was acquired by the Town Council in 1544 after the Dissolution of the Monasteries, and leased to the guilds, which adapted the buildings for their own uses. The complex has now been restored and houses craft workshops, permanent exhibitions illustrating Newcastle's development, a tourist information centre and restaurant.

The next day was back to work in a most enjoyable way, when I visited the MV *Logos*, a floating bookshop and missionary ship. The crew is made up of twenty-three different nationalities, and the project was started thirteen years ago with the aim of spreading the message of the Gospel. When I visited it, the ship had already sailed to seventy different countries, and in every port of call people are welcomed on board to buy books, chat and ask questions. The project director is an Australian doctor who gave up his practice in order to follow this new and overwhelming vocation. The project is funded entirely by voluntary donations, and it is an inspiration to see how this miniature floating United Nations, complete with families and children, live and work together, united by faith and missionary zeal.

In the Guildhall, centre of local government from the fifteenth to nineteenth centuries, I met one of the world's best-selling novelists, Catherine Cookson. This was to be my first big interview on the programme with someone outside my own profession, and I was pretty apprehensive about it. I knew that she had written more than sixty books — all except one of them about Tyne-side — but unfortunately I had not read any of them. For the first few moments of the interview we were both very nervous and Bill Ward, watching anxiously from behind the camera, began to wonder whether he had the right man for the job. So did I. We stopped filming and started again. I still hadn't got it right. Then I stumblingly asked the motherly, kind-faced novelist about her childhood days and suddenly it was like opening up a floodgate and she gave a wonderfully lucid description of those incredibly hard times, and everything clicked into place. Bill Ward put his thumb up and

Opposite top
Grey Street in the 1830s. It was then considered to be 'one of the most imposing façades in Europe'.

Opposite bottom
Blackfriars, one of the most complete Dominican Friaries surviving in Britain. Founded in the 13th century, it is now a crafts and exhibition centre.

Best-selling novelist, Catherine Cookson, the first person I interviewed for 'Highway'. She has written more than sixty books — all except one of them about Tyneside.

Below
The famous Tyne Bridge, the main road into the city. I kept looking for Sydney Opera House around the corner!

grinned. I heaved a big sigh of relief and, bringing the interview to a close, 'Thank you, Miss *Georgina Cookson*', I said.

The sea, of course, has played a vital part in New-castle's history, and in recognition of that fact we visited Trinity House and talked to the Master, Captain George Clark, who explained that this ancient guild of master mariners continues to look after the safety and welfare of the seafaring community. In the Chapel of Trinity House I sang with the Sinfonia Chorus one of my favourite hymns, 'He who would valiant be'.

The actor Peter Gilmore, who plays the redoubtable captain of 'The Onedin Line', read those memorable lines about the sea from Psalm 107:

> *They that go down to the sea in ships,*
> *that do business in great waters;*
> *These see the works of the Lord,*
> *and his wonders in the deep.*
> *For he commandeth, and raiseth the stormy wind,*
> *which lifteth up the waves thereof.*

The elegant Theatre Royal, a theatre I've not yet had the pleasure of playing — I wonder if they're trying to tell me something?

They mount up to the heaven,
they go down again to the depths:
their soul is melted because of trouble.
They reel to and fro, and stagger like a
drunken man, and are at their wits' end.
Then they cry unto the Lord in their trouble,
and he bringeth them out of their distresses.
He maketh the storm a calm,
so that the waves thereof are still.
Then are they glad because they be quiet;
so he bringeth them unto their desired haven.
Oh that men would praise the Lord for his goodness,
and for his wonderful works to the children of men!

There is something even more special about New-castle than its buildings and history, and that is the Geordie spirit, and the Geordie sense of humour. It's a spirit that permeates the city and its air of bustle and vitality, and underlies its vigorous refusal to be ground down by adversity, a character trait that was summed up for me in an extract from the writings of Geordie author Sid Chaplin. It was inimitably read by Tim Healy, of the television series 'Aufwiedersehen, Pet', when we did the 'Highway' programme from Jarrow.

People are only real in adversity. These people are real. So you take it or leave it. But I know one thing, I'm grateful and will always be grateful for a Geordie upbringing, a Geordie twang, and the Geordie sense of humour which has given me about sixteen million laughs against all the odds in this sad and sticky world.

And if ever I'm up against it — and I mean really fighting — I hope there's one voice around to shout: 'Gannon kidder, get stuck in'.

Then, win or lose, I should be ready to square my accounts.

DURHAM

For some people the North-East has the reputation of being a bleak part of these islands. They see it as an area of depression, suffering from the long-term effects of heavy industry. A place of pit-heads and colliery wheels, of belching chimney stacks and huge factories. Part of it does contain those elements but there are many areas of outstanding beauty. Take Durham, for instance. I had never been there before 'Highway' took me there, and to be honest I expected to find a grim city. But I was most pleasantly surprised. It's an extremely handsome city dominated by its cathedral where, incidentally, we spent all of our time on the programme, because it was a special edition for Remembrance Sunday. What a cathedral it is. It is unique. Standing on a red sandstone hill, its red-brown towers rise majestically up behind the walls of Durham Castle, themselves built sheer on the cliff edge above the River Wear. The cathedral dominates the town. It would take a book to recount its fascinating history and the way it has evolved over the centuries, but I shall confine myself to the extraordinary story of its founding, which is inextricably bound up with the story of St Cuthbert, the most famous saint of the north country.

Cuthbert was only a shepherd boy when he saw a vision of the soul of St Aidan being carried up to heaven by the angels, which inspired him to become a monk. He eventually became Bishop of the Holy Isle of Lindisfarne in 685; before he died two years later, he made his monks promise that if the Viking pirates came again, they would take his body with them wherever they went. Ten years after his death, Cuthbert's body was found to be without signs of decay, and was placed in a shrine. In 870 the Danish invaders came; when the monks opened Cuthbert's shrine the body was still as free from decay as on the day it had been buried, nearly

two hundred years before. The monks fled with the saint's body, and after eight years' wandering they settled at Chester-le-Street, near Durham.

For a hundred years the body was not disturbed again; then the Danes returned. Once more the monks fled with Cuthbert's coffin, and in 995 they came to Durham and, on a rocky piece of land surrounded on three sides by the River Wear, they built a little church of tree boughs over the sacred body as a temporary shelter until they could construct something stronger. In 998 this new building was dedicated, and the Saxon monastic community flourished there, St Cuthbert's shrine being a source of great wealth and prestige.

In 1071 William the Conqueror sent a Norman bishop to take over the order, but the men of Durham killed him and his followers. William and his army cruelly punished the whole of the area, leaving it a country of charred ruins. After this display of authority, Durham cathedral rose up under the direction of William de St Carileph (William of Saint-Calais), the real founder of the present cathedral. Vast and

Famous view of the Cathedral from the west. It stands on a seventy-foot high, wooded rock surrounded on three sides by the River Wear.

Opposite

Durham Cathedral, one of the most outstanding examples of Romanesque architecture in Europe, dates from the eleventh century.

The tomb of St Cuthbert, most famous saint of the North Country.

impressive, the Norman part of the building was completed in 1133; together with the castle which guarded the neck of the peninsula, it made an impregnable fortress before the days of the cannon; indeed Durham was the only city near the Border that was never taken by the Scots.

There is a story about Cuthbert and the Conqueror which I cannot resist retelling here. Bow Lane in Durham used to be called Kingsgate, so called apparently because William the Conqueror, while visiting Durham, demanded to see for himself whether St Cuthbert's body was really still not decayed. Before he could do so, he was seized with an 'excessive heat' which impelled him to depart from the cathedral in great haste and, leaping on to his horse, to ride off down Kingsgate and out of the city without waiting to enjoy the lavish entertainment that had been prepared for him.

Before we leave St Cuthbert I must just mention the fact that he did not like women; in fact women were never allowed even to approach his shrine in the cathedral — there is a line of black Frosterley marble beyond which they were not allowed to pass. In 1175, when Bishop Pudsey began building a Lady Chapel at the east end of the cathedral behind the saint's tomb, strange cracks appeared in the walls which were interpreted as signs of Cuthbert's disapproval — and the Lady Chapel (now called the Galilee Chapel) was built at the west end instead.

In 1540 the monastery at Durham was surrendered to Henry VIII and all its riches were confiscated. Cuthbert's shrine was broken open, and the saint's body was found to be 'whole, incorrupt, with his face

A view of the town from the River Wear. Circa 1890.

bare and his beard as it had been, a fortnight's growth, and all his vestments upon him as he had been accustomed to say Mass withal.' This description comes from the *Rites of Durham*, a day-to-day account of life in this great cathedral at the end of the Middle Ages. It was believed to have been written in 1593 by someone who had belonged to the monastery in his youth. St Cuthbert's body was finally laid to rest under a marble slab on the spot where his shrine had stood, and there it remains.

The vastness of Durham cathedral can be gauged from the fact that after the Battle of Dunbar in 1650, Cromwell incarcerated 4,000 Scots prisoners there, under the cruellest conditions, for upwards of two years. Having no coal with which to keep themselves warm, the prisoners broke up everything they could find that would burn. Many of them died during their imprisonment and were unceremoniously buried.

Amongst other interesting tombs, Durham Cathedral also contains the bones of the Venerable Bede, who completed his *Ecclesiastical History* in Jarrow monastery in 731. He was buried in Jarrow in 735, but about 1022 a monk called Aelfred stole the remains and brought them to Durham, where he was a sacrist. He had already accumulated a collection of relics of northern saints — it is to be hoped he had acquired the others by more respectable means.

Three things about the cathedral stand out in my mind: the first is the twelfth-century Sanctuary Knocker on the door below the north porch. Fugitives from justice had to knock with this to gain sanctuary, and for this purpose two monks were on permanent watch in the chamber above the porch. As soon as the sound of the knocker rang through the church, one of the monks would hurry down and admit the fugitive, and lead him to the sanctuary where he could safely remain for thirty-seven days. Then, if he had still not settled his affair he would be given a safe conduct to the coast. (I could not but irreverently reflect how useful such a knocker would have been in the wings of the old Glasgow Empire — many a comedian would gladly have sought refuge from the fearsome Scottish audiences they faced.)

The Galilee Chapel in the Cathedral. It probably got its name because it was the last stage of the Sunday Great Procession, which symbolized the return of Christ to Galilee.

The twelfth century Sanctuary Knocker on the door below the Cathedral's north porch. Fugitives from justice would knock with this in order to gain sanctuary in the Cathedral until their offences had been pardoned by the king. It is said to have secured asylum for over three hundred people between 1464 and 1524. They should have had one backstage at the Glasgow Empire!

The Miners' Memorial in the Cathedral. It is beautifully made of seventeenth-century Spanish woodwork with English Jacobean foliage and cherubs.

The second thing which particularly struck me is the memorial to the 12,000 Durham miners who gave their lives during World War I. It is beautifully made of seventeenth-century Spanish woodwork, with English Jacobean foliage and cherubs. The most poignant aspect for me, however, born in a mining community, was the simple miner's lamp which hung on the wall beside the memorial.

My third outstanding memory is of the Remembrance Garden of the Durham Light Infantry, where that splendid actress Wendy Craig, herself born and raised in a small mining village just outside Durham, read two moving poems by Christina Rosetti, both very appropriate for Remembrance Sunday.

Wendy Craig reads 'Remember' and 'Uphill' by Christina Rosetti in the Remembrance Garden. The most poignant reading we've had on 'Highway'.

REMEMBER

Remember me when I am gone away,
Gone far away into the silent land;
When you can no more hold me by the hand,
Nor I half turn to go yet turning stay.
Remember me when no more day by day
You tell me of our future that you planned:
Only remember me; you understand
It will be late to counsel then or pray.
Yet if you should forget me for a while
And afterwards remember, do not grieve;
For if the darkness and corruption leave
A vestige of the thoughts that once I had,
Better by far you should forget and smile
Than that you should remember and be sad.

UPHILL

Does the road wind uphill all the way?
Yes, to the very end.
Will the day's journey take the whole long day?
From morn to night, my friend.

But is there for the night a resting-place?
A roof for when the slow, dark hours begin.
May not the darkness hide it from my face?
You cannot miss that inn.

Shall I meet other wayfarers at night?
Those who have gone before.
Then must I knock, or call when just in sight?
They will not keep you waiting at that door.

Shall I find comfort, travel-sore and weak?
Of labour you shall find the sum.
Will there be beds for me and all who seek?
Yea, beds for all who come.

Wendy Craig went to the Durham High School for Girls, a church school connected with the cathedral, and she remembers sharing much of the life of the cathedral. Her particular inspiration in times of trouble now is the memory of her grandmother, a former headmistress of the village school, who went blind in her later years yet bore her affliction with stoicism and patience, and was an admirable example of how to cope with adversity. Despite being unable to see, she was determined to help with the war effort by knitting squares of khaki for blankets.

I have known Wendy for a long time and I'm proud to be a godfather to her son, Alastair, but even so I was very moved by the way she spoke about her grandmother and her father. She spoke lyrically of her wartime recollections as a child and I think that hers was one of the best interviews we have done on 'Highway'. I am gradually finding out that an interviewer's primary job is to listen to what his guest has to say and not interrupt. On this occasion I was delighted just to sit back and take in every word she had to say. Wendy Craig is a delightful lady and as lovely off screen as she is on it.

Bow Lane. It used to be called Kingsgate because, so the story goes, William the Conqueror, while visiting the town, demanded to see for himself the remains of St Cuthbert. But before doing so, he was seized with an 'excessive heat' which impelled him to ride off in great haste down Kingsgate and out of the city without waiting to enjoy the lavish entertainment that had been prepared for him.

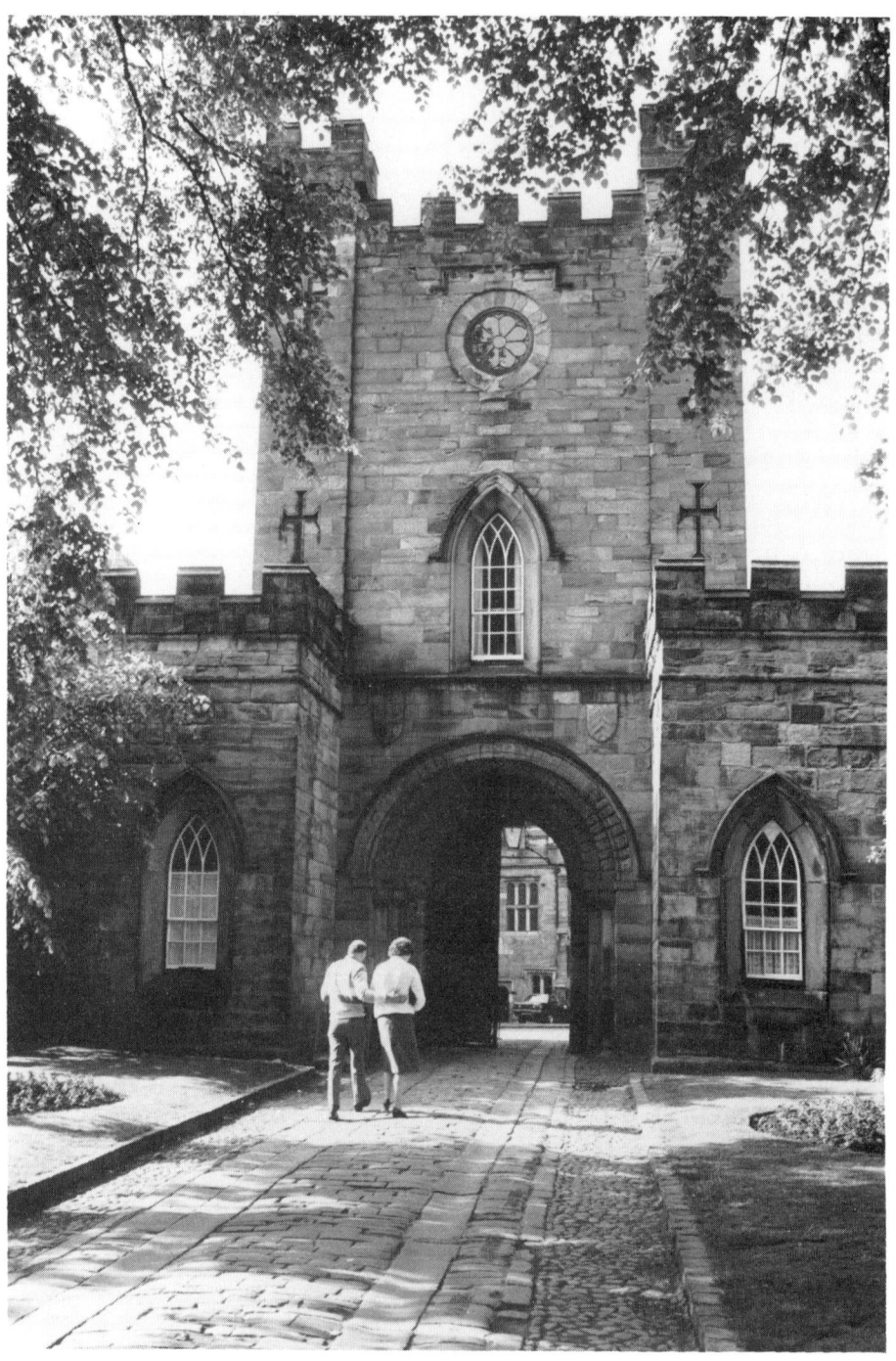

As you delve into the history of Durham you begin to understand the importance of the city to the kings of England. It suited them to have this powerful buffer between themselves and Scotland, and to have the power in the hands of non-hereditary bishops in whose appointment they had the last say, rather than in the hands of an ambitious family of nobles. From the Conqueror onwards, the kings of England bestowed great privileges upon the city, and the 'prince-bishops' were entitled to levy taxes, have their own exchequer, strike their own coins in their own mint, appoint their own judges to sit in their own courts, and so on. In return, the bishops were expected to maintain an army to repel the Scots, and to lead it if necessary.

The Norman castle, built about 1070, is now defending England no more. It is part of the University, which occupies most of the buildings in the old city centre. The first university in the north of England, it was founded in 1832 by the efforts of Bishop William van Mildert, the last Prince-Bishop of Durham. Its reputation now rivals that of Oxford and Cambridge.

Our brief in this particular 'Highway' programme was to commemorate the dead of two World Wars, without glorifying war, the supreme example of man's folly, and of his inhumanity to his fellow man. In the Chapel of the Durham Light Infantry, which was set up after World War I at the request of the officers to commemorate those who had fallen, we heard the regimental hymn, 'Abide with me', and were told by Archdeacon Hodgson that the chapel serves to remind us 'of those great qualities of sacrifice and loyalty and devotion to duty, and of the Regiment's motto, "Faithful", but when we look at this cross here which is from the First World War, it also reminds us that man has failed to live with his fellow man and has had to resort to war to solve his problems'.

Padre David Cooper's address to the victorious Falkland Islands troops went straight to the heart of the matter. When remembering their fallen comrades, he asked the soldiers also to 'remember what you felt when you thought you were going to die'. That surely brings home the true nature of war; its horrors, and its utter wastefulness.

The Norman Castle which occupies a commanding position in the town. Durham is unique among England's northern strongholds in that it never fell to the Scots. Part of the Castle is now used by the University.

Julian Lloyd Webber playing Bach's 'Ariosa'. We were all quite stunned with the brilliance of his playing.

Outside the cathedral, we ended the programme with a close-up of the rose which was dug up at Ypres by a young Lieutenant and transplanted wherever he went until, on his death, it was presented to the cathedral by his family. It is a cherished symbol of those who gave their lives in the world wars, whose memory we also cherish — not only on Remembrance Sunday, but always.

BRISTOL

When 'Highway' came to Bristol I felt on familiar ground again. Apart from having played Bristol Hippodrome on many occasions, it was a place I had often travelled through on my way down to Swansea in the days before I moved up to London to live. I remember vividly one time during the war returning through Bristol from leave. The train stopped in the Bristol Tunnel and there were rumours up and down the carriages about an air-raid in progress in the city. When we eventually emerged from the tunnel it was to discover Bristol in flames, and at Temple Meads Station all servicemen were ordered off the train to help put out the fires. I learned then how difficult it is to train a hose-pipe on a blaze. It's like trying to handle a boa constrictor. Anyway, we all did our best and eventually the fires were put under control and we were allowed to return to our units. It was an exhausting business, and I remember thinking at the time that it would take a long time to rebuild Bristol after all that devastation. Of course, it did take a long time and the city is not the same as it was then.

First, let's take a look at Bristol on the map. It stands at the confluence of the Avon and Frome rivers which unite within the city, and the combined stream (the Avon) runs into the Bristol Channel. Among the oldest seaports in the country, with a harbour in the heart of the city itself, Bristol has been a trading centre for over 900 years. In days of old it must have been a magnificent sight, with the masts of tall ships mingling with church spires as the vessels lay seemingly land-locked between the streets.

For the 'Highway' programme I sailed up the Avon, through the majestic Gorge, under Brunel's breath-taking Clifton Suspension Bridge — the first of its kind ever built, its 703-foot span a dizzy 245 feet above high

Isambard Kingdom Brunel's magnificent Clifton Suspension Bridge, the first of its kind ever built. I enjoyed the story of Sarah Ann Henley who, in 1885, driven by youthful despair over a lovers' tiff, jumped off but was gently parachuted by her petticoats to the mud below. She lived to be eighty-five!

water — and into Bristol's harbour. There are not so many merchant ships here now; commercial shipping has transferred to the modern docks at Avonmouth and Portishead. The City Docks have become a popular leisure area with a great many pleasure craft and cruising clubs, and a quayside complex called the Watershed which houses Radio West and an arts and shopping centre.

One of the sights of the City Docks is the SS *Great Britain*, another of Isambard Kingdom Brunel's achievements. The first ocean-going propellor-driven ship, she was launched in Bristol in 1843 by the Prince Consort, amidst great public excitement. The *Bristol Observer* described the scene thus:

> 'The day has been observed as a complete holiday. All the shops are shut, and business entirely suspended. Every church has displayed its flags, the ships have been dressed out in a variety of colours; peals have rung, and cannon fired; indeed every demonstration has been made that loyalty and rejoicing could inspire.'

It was in this blaze of glory that the *Great Britain* began her long sailing history. She spent the first thirty-one years of her life as a passenger ship, far outdoing the American sailing packets which had hitherto held a near monopoly of the North Atlantic passenger trade. During the following ten years she carried cargo only; in 1886 she was damaged at sea and beached in the Falkland Islands, where she was used as a storage vessel in Stanley Harbour until 1970, when she was towed home to Bristol to be restored in the very dock in which she was built. What an incredible saga!

Brunel was also the architect of the Great Western Railway, now of course more prosaically known as British Rail. However less romantic, the train now brings you from Paddington in little over an hour to this enchanting, richly historic city which has been a county since 1373 when it was constituted as such by Edward III. It was from this port that John Cabot and his son Sebastian set sail on a voyage which resulted in the discovery of the mainland of North America in 1497. Cabot subsequently became a life governor of the Company of Merchant Venturers, who under his

The exciting launch of the 3,433-ton *SS Great Britain* by the Prince Consort on 19 July, 1843.

direction tried to discover a way to China (or Cathay, as it was then known), by the north-east, an attempt which had important results for British trade with Russia and Asia. The Cabot Tower on Brandon Hill was erected in 1897 to commemorate the 400th anniversary of the explorers' setting-out, and it's a splendid vantage point for a view over the city.

Another famous native of Bristol was Thomas Chatterton (born 1752), the tragic boy poet who, obsessed with the Middle Ages and old documents, claimed to have found in an old chest in St Mary Redcliffe Church a paper entitled *A Description of the Friars' First Passing over the Old Bridge*. This he published in the *Bristol Journal* in 1768 when the new bridge at Bristol was completed. He also claimed to have found several poems (of equally spurious antiquity) which he attributed to one 'Rowley'. Unfortunately his forgeries did not long deceive his contemporaries; he was dismissed from his apprenticeship with a Bristol attorney, and left for London, but found no fortune there. He became destitute and, starving, poisoned himself in 1770 — in his eighteenth year.

Henry Wallis' painting of Thomas Chatterton, the tragic boy poet. Born in 1752 in the School House in Redcliffe where his father was a master, he spent many hours in St Mary Redcliffe Church reading the old manuscripts which inspired his medieval-style poems. He tried to make his fortune in London but became destitute and finally poisoned himself in his eighteenth year.

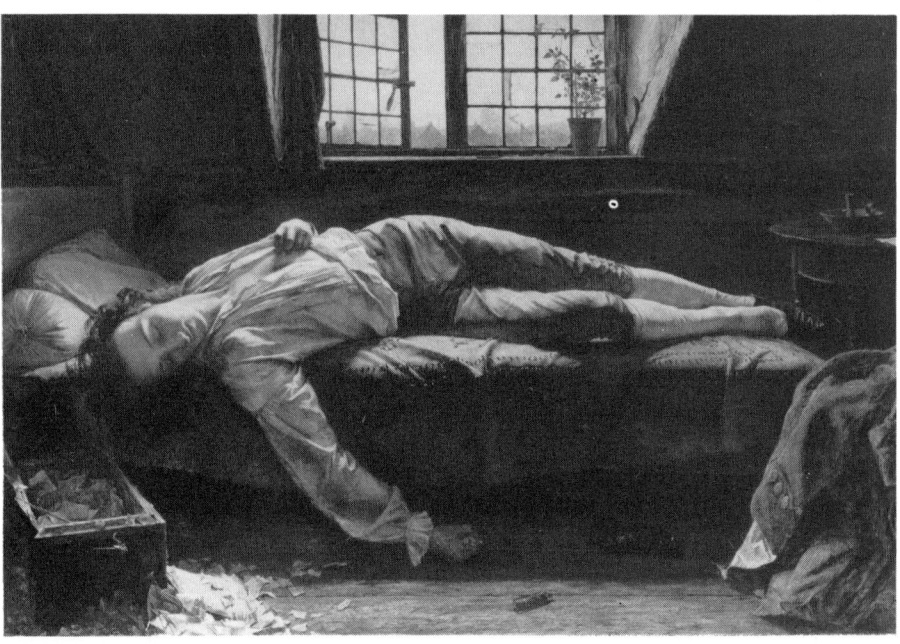

Opened in 1766, the Theatre Royal at Bristol is the oldest theatre in the country with a continuous existence. It has been the home of the Bristol Old Vic Company since 1946.

In my own particular professional sphere, I was fascinated by the Theatre Royal. Built in 1766, it is the oldest theatre in the country with a continuous existence. It may have new walls, but the attractive Georgian layout and decoration is still preserved. As for the standard of productions there, it is rightly considered to be one of the top theatres, and since 1946 has been the home of the Bristol Old Vic Company.

Mushrooming up from the pavement outside the eighteenth-century Exchange in Corn Street are the famous Bristol Nails, four bronze, flat-topped pillars on which the merchants put cash to settle their accounts — hence the saying, 'to pay on the nail'.

There's a fascinating Industrial Museum down in the City Docks, whose exhibits range from the definitive collection of Bristol-built aero-engines to a mock-up of the cockpit of Concorde, and there is also a waterside shunting engine which we used in the programme as a backdrop for Anita Harris to sing against. A Bristolian by birth, Anita is enthusiastic about the way the city planners have kept all the old 'magic', and integrated it with the best of the new. Incidentally, Anita is a very old friend of mine and it was a pleasure to work with her on the programme. We were together at the London Palladium in a revue and she has joined me on many trips abroad to entertain the Services — Singapore, Thailand and Borneo to name but a few exotic places.

A playbill for a 1799 performance at the Theatre Royal.

It was in the Industrial Museum that I met Derek Robinson, author of an indispensable phrasebook for non-Bristol speakers, entitled *Krek Waiters Peak Bristle*, otherwise interpreted as *The Correct Way to Speak Bristol*. As Derek Robinson so charmingly explained, 'We use the English language, but disguise it to baffle outsiders'. For example: GUARD NOSE (garden hose); LICE (lights). And if you've got them, you'll need a LICE WITCH (right — a light switch). Now you've grasped the idea, try this. One football player says to another, 'USURE RISE REF FEET RIPS ME AGAIN I LAMB RIM'. And the other player replies, 'EAT RIP DOVERS ZONE BOOTS REF'. And the soccer fan in the crowd shouts, 'GUESS TUCK INTERIM!' Simple, isn't it? The first player says, 'Use your eyes, ref. If he trips me again I'll hammer him'. And the other protests, 'He tripped over his own boots, ref'. And the fan shouts from the touchline, 'Get stuck into him!'

Actually, one thing I did learn from my visit generally is that it's a Bristolian habit to add an 'l' to the ends of words. The name of the town itself is a perfect example of this: in Saxon times it was called Bricgstow ('bridge-place'), but the 'l' was added to make it,

Opposite
The famous Bristol Nails: four bronze pillars on which merchants used to put cash to settle their accounts, hence the saying 'to pay on the nail'.

With Anita Harris. A great mate and a lovely lady to work with.

eventually, Bristol. Later in the programme I came across another instance. I was talking to local Transport & General Workers' Union leader, Ron Nethercott. He was telling me about a scheme he had to increase employment in the Bristol area. 'Oh yes', he said, 'it's a good ideal'. A good ideal it certainly was, but Ron was using 'ideal' for 'idea'. Ron Nethercott had intended to be a parson until William Temple, then Archbishop of Canterbury, and a man with a great social conscience, encouraged him to give up thoughts of a career in the church and instead follow his father into trade unionism, saying that he would touch more people's lives that way than he, Temple, did as Archbishop. As Ron Nethercott said, trade unionism isn't all about strikes; it's about caring for and kindness to one's fellow workers.

One of the things I was to learn while travelling around the country with 'Highway' is the extraordinary amount of local talent that flourishes everywhere, and I can't think of a better example than The Great Western Chorus who sang on the programme. This Bristol group started as a normal barbershop quartet, but is now 60-strong. I've always been a sucker for barbershop singing — coming from Wales I've been brought up to appreciate all kinds of choral singing — and I know that good barbershop singing is particularly hard to achieve.

The sixty-strong Great Western Chorus — plus one not so strong!

Firstly, the harmony is close harmony; you don't get the spread of harmony that you have in a normal male voice choir. Secondly, it is usually unaccompanied, and thirdly — and this is what really separates the men from the boys — good barbershop singing demands frequent chord changes, so that if one singer of the four is slightly out, it spoils everything. The Great Western Chorus have a natty uniform of checked plus-fours, bright red sweaters, and flat caps. They really look the part and sound sensational, and I enjoyed donning the outfit and joining their ranks for a song. Fortunately they didn't give me too much to sing. Their harmonies were so intricate, as I have said, that I was scared stiff of singing a 'bum' note. With a voice like mine, which has all the qualities of a laser beam, just one wayward note sticks out like a sore thumb. I really do admire those lads and I hope to get an opportunity to use them again.

In the beautiful church of St Mary Redcliffe, described by Queen Elizabeth I as 'the fairest, goodliest and most famous parish church in the kingdom', we heard internationally-renowned pianist Alan Schiller play Beethoven's 'Für Elise'. The church is an outstanding example of perpendicular architecture; it was founded in 1293, rebuilt in the fourteenth century by William Canynge the elder, and greatly enriched a century later by William Canynge the younger, one of the wealthiest of Bristol merchants, who eventually renounced all his worldly possessions to become a priest. He sang his first Mass in St Mary Redcliffe, an event commemorated every Whit Sunday by the Rush Sunday service, when the chancel floor is strewn with rushes in the medieval fashion, and the Lord Mayor and Corporation attend in full regalia.

I must just mention in passing one of Bristol's oldest pubs, the Llandoger Trow, which dates from 1664 and is said to have been the haunt of pirates and to figure in Robert Louis Stevenson's *Treasure Island*. What most appealed to me, in view of my earlier visit to King's Lynn and hearing about the fisherman Robinson Crusoe buried in St Nicholas' Chapel, is that the Llandoger is also said to have been the scene of interviews between Daniel Defoe and Alexander Selkirk, on whose real-life adventures Defoe based his novel

Opposite
St Mary Redcliffe with its graceful spire. Dating from the thirteenth century, it is one of the largest churches in England. Queen Elizabeth I described it as 'the fairest, goodliest and most famous parish church in the kingdom'.

The eighteenth-century Corn Exchange built by John Wood the elder. A training ground for young comedians!

Robinson Crusoe.

One of the less savoury aspects of Bristol's history is the part the city played in the shameful and highly lucrative slave trade.

More than eighty slave ships sailed out of Bristol during slavery's heyday, trading cheap gewgaws on the West African coast for slaves who were conveyed in appalling conditions to the West Indies, and there sold (as many as survived the horrendous voyage, that is) in return for rum, molasses and sugar. In a churchyard in

The headstones of the eighteen-year-old African slave, Scipio Africanus, at the churchyard in Henbury. Here are carved the poignant words: I who was born a pagan and a slave, Now sweetly sleeping, a Christian in my grave.

Opposite

John Wesley, founder of the Methodist Church. This statue stands outside John Wesley's New Room which, dating from 1739, was the first Methodist chapel.

the suburb of Henbury I saw a melancholy reminder of those days: the grave of an eighteen-year old African youth named Scipio Africanus. On his gravestone are carved the words:

'I who was born a pagan and a slave
Now sweetly sleeping, a Christian in my grave.'

One wonders what sorrows he had to bear in the process of becoming a Christian, far from his homeland and people.

Of course, many people thought the slave trade a good thing because it introduced Christianity to the 'pagans'; but one who spoke out vehemently against it was John Wesley, founder of the Methodist Church. In the centre of Broadmead, Bristol's new shopping centre which rose from an area devastated by wartime bombing raids, one building miraculously escaped destruction; John Wesley's New Room, the first Methodist chapel. It dates from 1739, and outside there is a statue of Wesley on horseback — a typical pose for a man who, it is estimated, rode a quarter of a million miles spreading the Word. He wrote hundreds of sermons in Bristol; the well-known actor Tony Britton appeared on 'Highway' to read extracts from two of them in Wesley's

own New Room. (Tony Britton's life has centred on Bristol for the past 45 years. As a schoolboy he remembers hearing the first German bombing raid on the Bristol Aircraft Corporation's factory at Filton — although he was 16 miles away from the spot. He could have given me a hand with the hosepipe if I'd known.)

This is an extract from Wesley's advice to young preachers:

'Be diligent. Never be unemployed. Never be triflingly employed. Never while away time.

Be serious. Avoid all lightness, jesting and foolish talking.

Converse sparingly and cautiously with women, particularly with young women.

Take no step towards marriage without solemn prayer to God and consulting your brethren.

Believe evil of no-one unless fully proved.

Speak evil of no-one.

Tell everyone what you think wrong with him, lovingly and plainly, and as soon as maybe, else it will fester in your own heart.

Do not play the gentleman.

Be ashamed of nothing but sin; no, not of cleaning your own shoes when necessary.

Be punctual. You have nothing to do but save souls.'

The following is the end of a sermon Wesley gave in a tiny upstairs room in Bristol, into which so many people had crowded to hear him that the floor gave way. The story goes that somehow or other the audience of staunch Bristolians stayed on to listen right to the end.

'Be not thou as other men are! Dare to stand alone. Let not custom or fashion be thy guide, but reason and religion. The practice of others is nothing to thee: every man must give an account of himself to God. Indeed, if thou canst save the soul of another do; but at least save one — thine own.

Walk not in the path of death because it is broad,

*and many walk therein. Nay, by this very token thou
mayest know it. Is the way wherein thou now
walkest, a broad, well-frequented, fashionable way?
Then it infallibly leads to destruction. Cease from
evil: fly from sin as from the face of a serpent!*

*Fall not short of a Pharisee in doing good. Give
alms of all thou dost possess. Is any hungry? Feed
him. Is he athirst? Give him drink. Naked? Cover
him with a garment. If thou hast this world's goods,
do not limit thy beneficence to a scanty proportion.
Be merciful to the uttermost of thy power. But rest
not here. Let thy religion be the religion of the heart.*

*Be serious: let the whole stream of thy thoughts,
words, and works be such as flows from the deepest
conviction that thou standest on the edge of the great
gulf, thou and all the children of men, just ready to
drop in, either into everlasting glory or everlasting
burnings! Be meek: let thy soul be filled with
mildness, gentleness, patience, long suffering toward
all men. Be thou a lover of God, and of all
mankind. Thus thou shalt be called great in the
kingdom of heaven.'*

'*Let thy religion be the religion of the heart*' : what an
inspiration those nine words are. If only we could all
live by them.

An 1870s engraving of
Bristol Cathedral.

97

SWANSEA

Never go back, that's what they say, isn't it, about places you've known and loved; to go back is to risk disappointment and disillusion. Of course I'd been back to Swansea many, many times since I took that first fateful journey from Swansea High Street to Paddington in search of fame and fortune. But this time I was going back to do the 'Highway' programme, and it meant suddenly looking at Swansea with fresh eyes. I had to distance myself from the town I've known since childhood, pull aside the veils of familiarity which have blurred perspectives and clouded judgements, try to peel away the many layers of memories, both happy and painful, which have overlaid reality and made objectivity almost impossible. In short, I had to separate the Swansea of my past from the Swansea of today.

My Swansea — the Swansea of my youth — was a warm, friendly town and, of course, it still is. The parts which featured prominently in my life, and, incidentally, in the programme — a fact which caused many ex-Swansea viewers to write rather angry letters to me complaining about bias, etc — were St Thomas, and Dan-y-Graig where I was born.

Dan-y-Graig Terrace was the scene of my first entry on to the stage of life — right on cue and in time for lunch, or dinner, as the midday meal was always called. It's a fairly nondescript street as streets go, running along the side of Kilvey Hill and overlooking the docks. In fact, my first childhood memories are of ships' funnels and the clanking of steam engines. The house in which I was born belonged to Mr and Mrs Roberts, and my parents rented two rooms in it. Cranfield's Bakery was a couple of doors away on one side and Fry's Fruit Shop was a few steps away on the other. The smell of baking bread and fresh oranges always takes me right back to my origins.

View of the St Thomas district of Swansea — the Swansea of my youth. We lived in the house attached to the bottom chimney in the picture — 7 St Leger Crescent.

Below

St Thomas from the docks with Kilvey Hill in the background.

St Leger Crescent was where we moved to when I was four. It formed part of a new council estate in St Thomas, the next district along to the west of Dan-y-Graig. Grenfell Park Estate stood on the grounds of a demolished manor house owned by the Grenfell family, hence its name. It sprawled along the lower slopes of Kilvey Hill, which along with Town Hill across the river, formed the two outstanding features of Swansea when seen from the sea. Life on the estate was fun — nobody had any money and neighbour borrowed cheerfully from neighbour. 'A cup of sugar'; 'A bit of cheese for our Tom's dinner box'; 'A couple of bob for the pictures'. It was useless to try to keep up with the Joneses — everybody was called Jones!

An area of the town — or city, as it now is — on which the programme did not touch is the Gower Peninsula, a spectacular place of castles and cliffs, sandy coves and beaches and miles of gorse and heather-covered hills. It was the first place in Britain to be designated an area of outstanding natural beauty, and a place where I spent many happy hours as a lad, both on organized Church outings and on trips on my own, riding my bicycle.

The spectacular Gower Peninsula, the first place in Britain to be designated an area of outstanding natural beauty.

It was a bicycle held together with bits of string, with brake blocks which were for ever popping out, a chain which was always coming off, and a saddle to make one's eyes water. But I loved it. I gave thirty bob for it, money hardly earned by making tea for the staff of Baldwins Colliery Department Head Office in Wind Street, an establishment in which I held the lowly position of Junior Pay Clerk. Making tea was an extra-curricular activity for which I charged the sum of a penny a cup — and good value it was, too.

This bicycle, this transport of delight, was my pass-port to freedom. No more asking for lifts on the crossbar from my more fortunate friends — my own wheels! I would pedal furiously across the landscape, calves bulging, shouting aloud my joy. Down plain streets named after Crimean Wars I would swoop. Sebastapol, Balaclava, Inkerman, head down against the wind, dew-drops from my nose smearing my glasses; free-wheeling one minute, legs pumping the next. I used to get cramp everywhere — even my eye-brows, where the muscles sometimes locked with my concentration, but I didn't care. The exhilaration was tremendous, and I saw more of the Gower than ever before or since. Parkmill, Pennard, Limeslade, even Rhossilly with its Worms Head and beautiful sandy beach. Oxwich, Brandy Cove, Three Cliffs Bay. Magic names for magic places. And they are all still there to be enjoyed.

Superficially Swansea is a new city, owing to the vast rebuilding programme undertaken since the war, when the town was extensively damaged. There are new shopping areas like the Quadrant and St David's Centre, new one-way traffic systems, new office blocks. Where is the old town? Where are the old buildings? The Swansea Empire? The Plaza Cinema? Of course I've known that they have been gone a long time; why then is it only now that I recognize the fact, with a shock of surprise? Is it because they've continued to exist in my mind, and it's only now when face to face with the present and reality that I suddenly notice their absence?

The Plaza was the last big cinema to be built in Swansea during my youth. It was truly grandiose, in keeping with its function of dispensing dreams, and its huge Grecian pillars proclaimed its connection with art

The Plaza Cinema where Myra and I met on our first date. It's got a lot to be responsible for!

and culture. It was there that I spent so many hours of my formative years, dallying with the sirens of the silver screen. You name a Hollywood star — Joan Crawford, Deanna Durbin, Olivia de Havilland — and I was in love with her. However, the Plaza was to play an even more important role in my life. When I returned from the war I went to a dance at the Mumbles Pier, splendidly attired in my demob suit. Across the room I spotted a petite, dark-haired beauty and, after removing my glasses for the sake of vanity and shyness — I asked her to dance and later walked her to the bus stop. I made a date to meet her at six o'clock the following evening outside the Plaza Cinema.

The next day, at a quarter to six, I positioned myself strategically behind one of the Plaza's pillars in such a way as to be invisible to anyone approaching from the front — six years of army service had not been without its uses. For the life of me I couldn't remember what the girl had looked like, and I didn't trust my short-sighted first impression. I decided to await the arrival of the dark stranger and if she was as beautiful as I had first believed I would emerge from my hiding place and gallantly make myself known to the lucky girl. On the other hand, should I find I had made a big mistake, I would remain hidden behind my pillar until she had departed.

Six o'clock came, but brought no dark beauty with it. Nor had she appeared by 6.15. At 6.30, in the humiliating knowledge that it was I who had been stood up, I emerged, a much-chastened man from behind my pillar . . . just as my dark-eyed beauty emerged from another one. It was Myra (who else?) and we both laughed and have continued laughing together ever since.

I began the 'Highway' programme in a very appropriate place; the new theatre in the docks that was recently opened to commemorate perhaps Swansea's most famous son, the poet Dylan Thomas, who painted a vivid picture of the town in just a few words:

> '. . . an ugly, lovely town, crawling, sprawling,
> slummed, unplanned, jerry-villa'd and smug
> suburbaned by the side of a long and splendid
> curving shore.'

I had the privilege of opening the Dylan Thomas Theatre, and I'll tell you one thing for sure: Dylan would have been delighted with it, built as it is on the site where Oscar Chess's garage once stood. It isn't all plush and grand, it isn't lavishly equipped backstage with modern equipment and glamorous dressing-rooms, but the simplicity of the place ensures that the words get across, and words were Dylan's stock-in-trade. It is also not a theatre which opens only at night. It is a thriving, vital community and social centre where anyone with a project is welcome to use the facilities.

The docks I knew have gone. The big cranes which used to load the coal are no more, and down where I used to wander, looking at the boats, they've got a Transport Museum and a Leisure Centre. One of the exhibits in the museum is part of a Mumbles Train. The famous Mumbles Railway used to connect Swansea

with Mumbles Head, winding on a scenic route along the coast. There is an exhibition of photographs in the museum and on one of them I was delighted to see my Uncle Cyril — my father's brother. He was an inspector on South Wales Transport for many years and was one of the reasons for my going into show business. My father's youngest brother, he was always the life and soul of any party and when I was a boy he was my idol. He could play the ukelele, the banjo and, of all things, a musical saw. He used to place it between his legs and hit it with a drumstick, producing a sound remarkably like a soprano singing. How he did it I don't know, but it certainly looked dangerous.

At the end of the first day's filming I arrived back at the hotel elated, to be greeted by Myra who had been to see her Aunty Elsie, who still lives in Swansea.

'How many were in your class at school?' she asked me.

Myra has a wonderful habit of asking a question in a way that is half statement and half interrogation, with a little touch of accusation thrown in for good measure.

'Oh, the usual number', I answered, thinking it was a bit of an odd question. 'Somewhere between twenty-five and thirty. Why do you ask?'

'Oh, it's just that this afternoon I've met at least fifty men who claim they were in your class at school', said Myra dryly. 'Not to mention an old woman who used to rub goose-grease on your chest when you were a baby'.

The next day we went on one of those visits that make 'Highway' different from any other programme I've known. It was to Tŷ Olwen.

It's strange how some words can take on a terrible power. 'Cancer' is one. It can induce dread and hope-lessness in the stoutest heart, and the fact that the fight against the disease is now on a more equal footing seems to have done nothing to lessen the evocative power of that word. 'Hospice' is another such word; that, we have come to believe, is where the terminally ill die. Forget the word, and anyway it's not even a true definition.

Tŷ Olwen is run by a remarkable man: Dr Peter Griffiths, who gave up a successful medical practice of

Outside the Dylan Thomas Theatre. The first to be named after him.

With Dr Peter
Griffiths, the Medical
Director of Tŷ Olwen.

some twenty years' standing to become the head of Tŷ
Olwen. Dr Griffiths describes the place as 'a continuing
care unit, for people with advanced malignant disease,
in which active treatments aimed at a cure are no longer
appropriate. People believe that a terminally-ill patient
can last three days or three weeks; well, he can also last
three years, and it is our job to keep any patient
symptom-free, with the methods we have at our
disposal, living in comfort with his family'. The targets
set in Tŷ Olwen — the 'realizable goals' — sound
modest, and yet they represent 'large victories': 'A day
at home for one patient. A week for another. Staying
alive for a niece's wedding, or long enough to see again a
son returning from Australia'.

Dr Griffiths took me around the unit, and I found it
a stimulating and inspiring experience. It was also a
happy and cheerful one, with much laughter and good
humour among the patients. The only problem I
encountered was when a dog ran under my feet and I
almost tripped over.

'I've never seen a dog in a hospital ward before', I
told Dr Griffiths.

'Oh yes', he said, not in the least bothered. 'We encourage patients to bring any special pets in with them.'

I left Tŷ Olwen just before the cocktail hour — yes, really. The patients drink what they like. At the risk of advertising, Guinness seems to be particularly popular.

The next day we went to Swansea Market, the largest covered market in Wales, built where the old one used to be, at the back of the old Swansea Empire. I couldn't visit Swansea without buying some cockles, freshly gathered on Gower's north coast at Penclawdd, and some laverbread, which is made from an edible sea-weed and is absolutely delicious fried with bacon. The new market is splendid and airy, and has its share of characters among the stallholders: you are as likely to be offered some free philosophy with the fruit or fish that you buy as some anecdotes of Swansea's ancient history.

Swansea Market used to be Aladdin's Cave to me when I was a little boy. It contained everything any boy ever dreamed of possessing. Footballs, real leather ones, hung from the tops of stalls along with football boots slowly swinging in tied pairs, studs glistening in the lamplight. Mounds of marshmallows, hard-boiled sweets in the shape of goldfish and pineapples, and pear drops, mushrooms made of coconut, and marzipan provided enough saliva in an impressionable lad to create a Salivation Army.

My mother used to take me there on Saturday afternoons to help carry the weekend shopping bags home, because it was a long haul up St Leger Crescent from the tram stop at the bottom of Margaret Street by the church. When she had chosen her purchases, something she always took her time over, chatting to the stallholders, feeling the vegetables, prodding the chickens, but rarely buying one — they were too expensive then — we would thread our way through the throng of shoppers, loud-voiced from the Valleys, posh-voiced from Sketty and the Uplands, caps and scarves, trilbies and headscarves, past the cockle women, jolly and red-faced, making jokes in Welsh about the passers-by; and into one of the white-tiled booths around the periphery of the market for faggots and peas. And I

Swansea market at the turn of the century. A place to make a young lad drool at the mouth.

would thankfully put the bags down, fingers criss-crossed with red lines from the string handles, the steam from the faggots fogging my glasses. 'Eat up, now, there's a good boy for your Mam'.

Max Boyce is a lively, lovely lad. He has the lilt of the valleys in his voice and is as sunny a character as you'll ever find — except when Wales loses at Rugby. Then he become almost suicidal. He takes Wales with him wherever he goes, becoming a rallying point for expatriates in the far-flung 'Empires' he sings in. The only trouble that day in Swansea Market was the fact that Myra and I couldn't really get a chance to chat with him. There were so many people asking for auto-graphs and patting him on the back and patting me on the head — I'm shorter than he is — that it was impossible to have a proper conversation. Pity, because he knows more good Welsh jokes than anybody, and I could use a few.

At the bottom of St Leger Crescent stood — and still stands — St Thomas Church. I once described it as a lean greyhound of a church looking down with haughty Anglican dignity on the non-conformist mongrels of Port Tennant Road. It was here that I served my time as a choirboy and I was delighted when Caroline Burne-Jones, the director, decided to feature it in the programme.

Max Boyce, the playboy of the Western Mail, eating cockles in the market-place.

It was a rather eerie experience to return to a place where I had spent so many hours of my youth — singing hymns lustily, nodding and frowning with apparent concentration during the sermon, looking angelic in the rays of the late evening sun shining, mote-dappled, through the stained-glass windows, and all the time I was off exploring Africa or shooting tigers in India or scheming out a way to take Glenys to the pictures.

A lot of things had changed in the church but it was essentially as I remembered it. The hook where I used to hang my cassock and surplice, the same musty smell in the vestry — why do all church vestries smell the same? The choir was different too, because I was joined by the Morriston Orpheus for the occasion and a jollier bunch of lads you've never met. If our choir master, Mr Ward, had had them for his own he would have challenged the Mormon Tabernacle Choir to a

With Mary Hopkin who sang 'The Coming of the Roads'. Lovely to look at and lovely to listen to.

Opposite

St Thomas Church where I sung as a choirboy. The drainpipes were once painted by me — the wrong colour!

111

With the Morriston Orpheus Choir, one of the best-known Welsh male voice choirs. This photograph was taken inside St Thomas Church on the spot where I sang my first solo ever.

Opposite

Our wedding day. I'm the one on the left!

singing contest and won hands down. It was a most rewarding experience to sing with them and I shall always cherish that evening in St Thomas Church, where on the same spot that I had sung trembling solos as a boy, I sang my heart out with the Morriston Orpheus.

Afterwards we all had tea and sandwiches in the church hall and I was able to renew a lot of old friendships amongst the lady helpers, some of whom had been in the choir when I was a member. A great night altogether.

One of the nicest things about going back to Swansea is that I'm treated as if I've never been away, but then, that is only what I would expect. Welsh people are so uncomplicated, natural and friendly. Although some people have been bothered by my knighthood, not being very sure how to address me, Swansea people have no such difficulty: Harry Secome I was, and Harry Secombe I remain. It's Myra who has the problem. The bill from the Dragon Hotel was addressed to Sir Harry and Mrs Secombe. Eat your heart out, Myra!

BELFAST

Opposite top

The Victorian Grand Opera House. It has recently been renovated, and artists from all over the world perform there. I played there in 1951 — I don't think they understood a word I said!

It was a strange feeling, flying off to Belfast; there was a perceptible heightening of tension, although I expected no trouble. In any event, it was going to be different from the many other trips I had made to Northern Ireland since the Troubles began. These usually consisted of one night stopovers in Belfast or Londonderry — or as it is now officially known, Derry — when there was no opportunity for exploring and discovery, and it was a case of airport, hotel, concert, hotel, airport and 'Hello Myra'. At least this time I'd have enough leisure to behave like an ordinary tourist.

There were, of course, special circumstances and particular problems connected with Northern Ireland which we didn't meet with in any of the other places we visited. Some viewers took us to task for seemingly ignoring these; but to accuse us of doing so is to misunderstand the aims of 'Highway'. We knew full well that the outwardly composed and peaceful veneer that we encountered concealed festering sores of hatred and unrest, but it was not part of the programme's brief to highlight such problems. That is surely the province of the documentary film, which specializes in political reportage and in-depth analysis. It would have been supremely arrogant for us to pass judgement, or to believe that in a fleeting three-day visit we could even begin to understand the depths of the dispute. 'Highway' seeks to bring some degree of solace and comfort, and that was our aim in each of our visits to Northern Ireland.

Opposite bottom

I spent a cheerful half-hour with some of the city's dockers. They still didn't understand a word I said!

I cannot pretend that I came away feeling vastly encouraged, but equally I would not be telling the whole truth if I neglected to say that there do exist cases of hope and encouragement. Certainly one is inclined to have a false picture of everyday life in Belfast, our only yardstick being the news coverage given to the

The city dockland area showing the Queens and Queen Elizabeth Bridges over the River Lagan. Ship-building is still a major industry in Belfast.

sectarian violence that has gone on for fifteen years or more in a city which, according to the pictures on our television screens, is constantly patrolled by soldiers.

Let me say categorically that I didn't see a single soldier while I was there to do 'Highway'. The time was a few weeks before Christmas, and Belfast was a busy, bustling city preparing for the festive season to come in a way that would be hard to differentiate from any city on the mainland. Of course, there were differences; for instance, on the road to the airport there are an inordinate number of 'sleeping policemen', clearly to discourage — if not render quite impossible — an attack by any form of motorized transport. Another difference was evident when we approached the Conway Hotel, and had to leave our taxi and go through the 'guard room' for a security check. The hotel itself is set in beautiful grounds, but is somewhat incongruously surrounded by a high wire fence.

It took me some time to realize that while such things appeared unusual to me, as far as the people of Northern Ireland are concerned, their 'eye was in', so to speak. What we regarded as strange, they have sadly become used to. On this, and other visits, when our taxi was stopped by an armed policeman, the driver took it in his stride. For him it had become par for the course.

Like so many other cities, Belfast developed dynamically as a result of the Industrial Revolution. The growth of industries such as linen and rope-making, ship-building and tobacco doubled the size of the town every ten years, and today one in three of the population of Northern Ireland lives in this city of some 400,000 people.

For the opening of the programme, a barge brought me down the River Lagan, right into the heart of the Belfast Harland and Wolff shipyard. Ship-building has always been a major industry: here the *Titanic* was

The waterways have always been vital to trade. Imported goods used to be transported by horse-drawn barges down the River Lagan.

Dancers performing in the entrance hall at Queen's University added a traditional Irish flavour to the programme.

built, and here too is the world's biggest dry dock. The river and waterways were things of beauty, but still vital to trade, and thousands of tons of imported goods used to be transported picturesquely by horse-drawn barges. Sadly, today, the river is suffering from the all-too-familiar ravages of industry and pollution, but the beauty still shines through.

I went upstream from the shipyard to find the tranquil surroundings of Queen's University. The main building is very fine, with its mellow brickwork and mullioned windows. It was modelled on Magdalen College, Oxford, and was built in 1849 by Charles Lanyon, who designed more distinguished buildings in Belfast than anyone before or since. The music faculty and the University concert hall are named after Ireland's most famous composer, Sir Hamilton Harty, 'the Irish Toscanini', a brilliant interpreter of Romantic music.

I am constantly amazed at the way the strong traditions of song and dance still flourish in Northern Ireland and Scotland. There are literally hundreds of small bands in the province of Ulster who, with flutes and accordion keep alive the songs and melodies of the people. We were privileged to watch traditional Irish dancers perform to the music of the Fluters Five, and I was struck by the similarity between the Irish choreography and Scottish dancing, as well as the kind of Welsh dancing I've often admired at Eisteddfod.

At the beginning of this chapter I mentioned certain cases of hope that we encountered in Belfast. I'd like to mention three of them here. Two out of the three concern young people, because it is with the young that the main hope of the province for a peaceful future lies.

The largest grammar school in the British Isles is to be found in Belfast, at Methodist College — known locally as Methody. It has over two thousand students, and when it celebrated its centenary in 1968 a new chapel was opened there. Called the Chapel of Unity, it is just that: a place for all denominations, and just as importantly, for people of none. It is a place of reason as well as place of worship, and the fact that the children of Methody are being educated in a school which actually practises tolerance rather than just preaching it, gives ground for cautious optimism.

The Chapel of Unity seemed the perfect place to meet marriage counsellor, Roy Simpson, who told me, rather to my surprise, that the additional pressures of Northern Ireland's political problems seemed not to be a factor contributing to the breakdown of marriages in Ulster. In fact, statistics show that marital breakdowns are brought about in Northern Ireland and the rest of Britain by exactly the same kind of problems — lack of communication, economic and social difficulties, sexual and family problems. However, though broken marriages are on the increase, Roy Simpson told me that marriage, far from going out of fashion, has never been more popular. This was my second oasis of hope. Roy Simpson sees his job as advising with humanity; he is not concerned to save a marriage at all costs, but rather to ensure that those which must break up do so with the minimum of hurt to all involved.

The third oasis of encouragement was provided by a group of young children from the Harpers Hill County Primary School, who with their choir and steel band gave a performance of sublime enthusiasm and freshness, and whose utter innocence gave all of us a positive glow of hope for their future.

It had been a full day's work, and I was looking forward to the next day, when I would be free to explore. I started with a drive round the city, admiring its many Victorian and Edwardian buildings, but had

The Main Street in the delightful small town of Hillsborough about ten miles south of Belfast which I visited. Many of the town's antique shops and pubs are in fact fine Georgian townhouses.

decided that since my time for visiting was so limited, I would spend most of my time outside the city.

Travelling by car in Northern Ireland is a joy. Quite apart from the panorama of beautiful scenery, it is so wonderful these days to find roads that are practically empty of traffic — the only jams you are likely to encounter are flocks of sheep and cows changing fields. I drove to Hillsborough, a delightful small town about ten miles south of Belfast. The steep main street is lined with antique shops and pubs, many of them formerly Georgian town-houses. Sir Hamilton Harty is buried in the graveyard there.

After a very satisfactory lunch (which I had difficulty in squaring with my diet sheet!) I drove north-east of Belfast, to the Ulster Folk and Transport Museum at Cultra. I am never entirely besotted with museums that show disconnected relics of the past, perhaps because I'm lacking in imagination. The museum at Cultra is something different; it is in fact in so many ways exactly what I think a museum should be: a place where you can really visit the past. Here you can see a flax mill, a smithy, an old weaver's house, even a schoolhouse furnished with old desks and reading books. All these buildings have been carefully dismantled, stone by stone, and just as carefully rebuilt inside the museum. In the summer you can see demonstrations of weaving, spinning and thatching there.

The old schoolhouse which I visited at the Ulster Folk and Transport Museum, Cultra.

Crafts being
demonstrated at the
Ulster Folk and
Transport Museum:
right, a spademaker;
far right, a blacksmith.
Below: the spade mill.

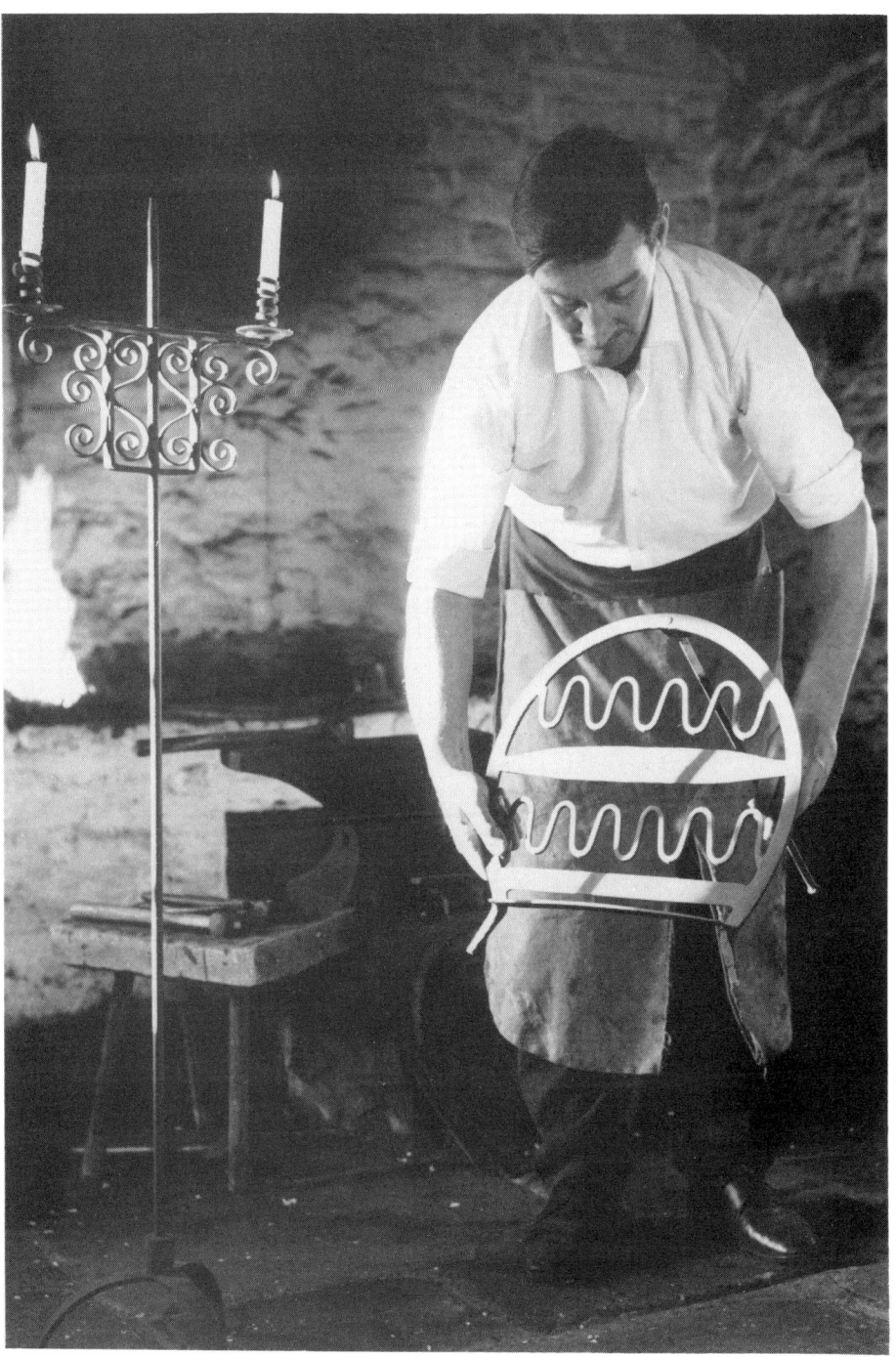

From Cultra I drove to the other side of Belfast Lough to visit Carrickfergus, with its massive Norman castle, built by John de Courcy in 1180. In the seventeenth century Carrickfergus was the only place in Northern Ireland where English was spoken, Gaelic then being the language of Ulster. At the delightfully-named Boneybefore, a plaque marks the ancestral home of a former American president, Andrew Jackson, and Jonathan Swift, writer of *Gulliver's Travels,* was prebendary of a church nearby.

The next day we were filming in the centre of Belfast in front of the City Hall with its statue of Queen Victoria. The area was thronged with pre-Christmas shoppers, and in addition to them the television cameras were attracting their usual quota of sightseers,

Carrickfergus Castle. The first real Irish castle. It was built in 1180 to guard the approach to Belfast Lough at Carrickfergus.

but everyone felt absolutely secure. Not a soldier was to be seen, nor did there seem to be any policemen in evidence to control the good-humoured crowds. We were delighted to show this on the programme; as they say, one picture is worth a thousand words.

The City Hall in the centre of Belfast.

We were amply entertained by singer Candy Devine, an unusual lady to find in Belfast because she was born and raised in North Queensland, Australia. However, she came to Belfast to sing in cabaret, and liked it so much she never went home. She even married a Belfast man. The crowd joined in with her and the band, while I talked to ex-Lord Mayor Tom Patton. He was concerned about Belfast's image on the mainland: 'Everyone seems to be under the impression that we're all running about toting guns', he said. 'They think the people of Belfast don't live a normal, everyday life. That's why I'm delighted to see you here.'

The lovely Candy
Devine. Queensland's
loss is Belfast's gain.

Below

With comedian Frank
Carson — playing
book-ends!

Comedian Frank Carson was also there. 'I was born in Corporation Street down by the docks', he told me. 'That's where all the cheap wine came in. I think it was about tuppence a gallon. It tasted like varnish. You died a horrible death — but you had a lovely finish!'

It was time to leave Belfast. It was hard to think that soon we would be back in London, and almost inevitably we would hear news of yet another shooting or bombing incident somewhere in this beautiful province of Northern Ireland, which could easily be so prosperous. Yet we knew with a dreadful certainty that the light of peace was not yet visible at the end of Ulster's long, dark tunnel.

I thought again of C.S. Lewis's wonderful poem, *The Nativity*, which had been read during the programme by Kevin Flood, and wished with all my soul that we could all win some of that 'woolly innocence' the poet speaks of:

> *Among the oxen (like an ox I'm slow)*
> *I see a glory in the stable grow*
> *Which, with the ox's dullness might at length*
> *Give me an ox's strength.*
>
> *Among the asses (stubborn I as they)*
> *I see my Saviour where I looked for hay;*
> *So may my beastlike folly learn at least*
> *The patience of a beast.*
>
> *Among the sheep (I like a sheep have strayed)*
> *I watch the manger where my Lord is laid;*
> *Oh that my baa-ing nature would win thence*
> *Some woolly innocence!*

ABERDEEN

'Could we have that opening link once again?' asked the ever-cheerful floor manager.

'What was wrong with it?' I asked.

'Nothing really. It's just that Alan thought you looked a little tense.' (Alan was Alan Franchi, the director and producer of the Aberdeen episode of 'Highway'.)

A little tense? I thought to myself. Now why should that be? Here I was, alone on the deck area of the oil-platform known as Forties Charlie, an 80-mile-an-hour, bitingly cold North Sea gale was threatening to blow me off my feet, laughing itself silly about my thermal underwear, and if I slipped or was blown by the wind there was no protective guard rail to stop me falling into the North Sea. But not to worry if I did — true, you can only survive two minutes in that icy sea in winter, but a boat circles the platform twenty-four hours a day to take care of such eventuality.

All in all, I thought, no reason whatever to feel tense.

'Five seconds!' called the floor manager, and I tried to prise my upper lip clear from where it was sticking to my teeth.

I performed my opening link again.

'How was that?' I asked.

'That was fine', came the reply. 'But Alan would like just one more. You said "oil-rig", not "oil-platform".'

'Silly me', I said, with the falsest laugh this side of Cwmllynfell. As every schoolboy knows, an oil-rig is where the actual exploration for oil takes place; an oil-platform is where it is 'milked' from the sea-bed to an on-shore base.

The next take did it, and very thankfully I went below. Now, approaching Las Vegas by air is a weird experience. For hours it seems that you have been flying

Forties Charlie oil-platform in the North Sea. Since the 1960s when oil was first discovered in the North Sea, it has become a major industry in Aberdeen. The lads working on these rigs deserve all the money in the world. It's a tough job, believe me.

Castle Street, circa 1812. From an engraving by C. Turner after a painting by Hugh Irvine.

over completely arid desert, and then suddenly, in the midst of nowhere, just like a mirage, this unbelievable city materializes. Approaching Forties Charlie is rather similar. We flew by helicopter and all that could be seen was the angry, ever-turbulent sea below. Then suddenly a dot appeared on the horizon. It grew bigger as we headed towards it, and suddenly there it was, this tiny, man-made floating island, one hundred and ten miles out from the shore.

Willing hands helped us alight; and though we had been warned that it was going to be cold, none of us was expecting anything as cold as this.

The oil-platform works twenty-four hours a day, extracting its black treasure from the sea-bed, nine thousand feet below the platform. The men work a 12-hour day, 14-day shifts, alternating with 14 days ashore. Long working hours and unsociable conditions are made bearable by the knowledge, as one worker put it, that their time on the platform is limited — that and the fact that once they're there, there's no getting off!

There is a strict rule about no alcohol aboard, and there is a noticeable lack of women, but the wages are good and life is made as comfortable as possible for the men. Take food, for example. Not only is it plentiful, but the canteen offers a menu that would be the envy of many a West End restaurant. Let me put it this way, stuck with my diet, I found more food there that I wasn't allowed to eat than in any hotel I'd yet stayed in during the course of the 'Highway' series.

Unfortunately, television reception is very poor on the platform, but there is a vast library of videos to be drawn upon. There is also a well-equipped library. Card games abound, and there is of course conversation. Being strangers on the platform we were the centre of attention, and I enjoyed meeting a lot of new people.

An aquatint of Aberdeen by William Danniell (1769-1837) for his 'Picturesque Voyage Round the Coasts of Great Britain'.

Particularly one.

'Your accent's familiar', I said. 'Where are you from?'

'Swansea', he said.

'I'm from Swansea', I said.

'I know', he said.

'I'm there next week', I said, 'doing "Highway".'

'I know', he replied again.

'I'm singing with the Morriston choir', I said.

'Yes, I know', he replied yet again.

This was too much. 'Perhaps you can tell me what I'm singing', I enquired, a trifle sarcastically.

'Yes', he said. '"Swansea Town" and "Eli Jenkins' prayer".'

'That's right', I said, weakly. 'How did you know?'

'Because I'm in the choir and I'll be there on leave'.

True enough, the next time I saw him he was in St Thomas Church in Morriston.

The 'Granite City' seen from the air. Helicopters journey back and forth between the shore and the oil-platforms.

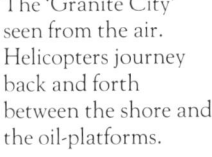

But back to the oil-platform. No matter how careful the planning, emergencies do sometimes arise, particularly in matters of health. Often a sick person must be hospitalized, and quickly. It is then that the wonderful helicopter service comes into its own. These craft and their crew will land and take off in the cruellest of weather, usually performing feats of heroism as part of the day's work.

If the oil-platform had a signature tune, I'm sure it would be that Rodgers and Hammerstein classic, 'There is nothing like a dame', for on all but the rarest of occasions there is nothing like a dame to be found on Forties Charlie. In our party we had Isla St Clair, who comes from the north-east of Scotland, and who has been singing folk-songs since before she even knew what folk-songs were. She entertained us with a folk-song about whaling, which used to be carried on from that part of Scotland.

The following day, when the weather cleared, the ever-faithful helicopter was on hand to whisk us back to Aberdeen. The pilot made a detour so that we could enjoy the sight of the 'Granite City' from the air. We could easily appreciate an Aberdonian's pride in his 'fair city of the rivers twain', sandwiched between the Don and the Dee. Scotland's third largest city, Aberdeen's recorded history dates from the twelfth century, when it was already a Royal Burgh; and in 1319 the Great Charter of Robert the Bruce conferred great privileges on the town in return for the citizens' support during his struggle against Edward I, the Hammer of the Scots. They not only sheltered him and fought for him at the Battle of Burra, but it is reputed that they slew the English army garrisoned in Aberdeen Castle. The Bruce's daughter even married the Town Clerk, one Thomas Isaac.

The oil boom has brought great prosperity to the city; the diesel trawlers that were once Aberdeen's most important indigenous industry have fallen victim to recession, but the harbour has never been busier, with a host of oil-rig supply craft that service the North Sea oil fields.

We landed on the heli-pad at Aberdeen Royal Infirmary, whose Premature Baby Unit is a source of great

pride not only to the hospital but to the city. The unit's team is headed by Dr David Lloyd, who took me to see the premature baby ward. Looking at those tiny little babies I marvelled anew at God's greatest miracle, life itself; somehow it seemed doubly miraculous in such minute scraps of humanity. What I found so inspiring about Dr Lloyd was his emphasis not so much on the wonders of technology, but on the importance of love and caring in the work of the Unit, and particularly the love of parents, grandparents and even brothers and sisters, all of whom are encouraged to be involved with the baby and to participate in caring for it. Families are encouraged to do as much as possible, even to the extent of tube-feeding their tiny offspring.

Opposite
The harbour which has been central to the town's prosperity since the twelfth century. Today, the colourful oil supply vessels which service the North Sea predominate here.

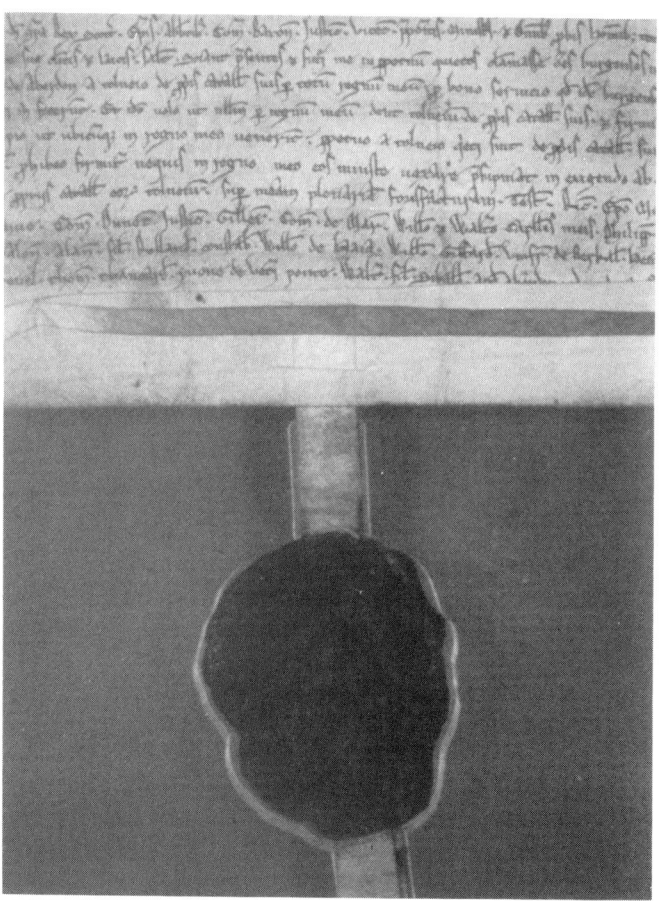

The 1319 Great Charter of Robert the Bruce which conferred many privileges on the town in return for the citizens' support during his struggles against Edward I.

'Our emphasis is on caring', said Dr Lloyd. 'The thing that we are here to do is to show not only parents but our medical staff how to care for babies'.

The earliest baby delivered at the Unit was sixteen weeks premature, and had had a gestation time of only 24-25 weeks inside the mother. I saw the most miraculous treatment being administered to a baby while I was there. Dr Lloyd told me that it required help with its breathing for the first few days of its life, and that was the reason for the kind of space bubble over its head as it lay in the incubator. Oxygen was being administered through this hood so that the baby could breathe. In addition, the baby had various leads attached to a heart rate monitor, and through these special electrodes the staff were able to assess the levels of oxygen and carbon dioxide in the baby's blood.

I found the visit a very moving experience, but was saddened to learn that the hospital has been told to expect to have its allocation of funds reduced, owing to the cuts in the National Health Service.

Before we left the hospital we heard the Bon Accord Silver Band play, as they often do, for the patients. (Bon Accord, by the way, was the rallying cry of the Bruces.)

At the hotel that evening I asked for advice on what I should see the following day, and I knew I was in Scotland when I was told in no uncertain terms that the way to see Aberdeen was 'to walk, laddie'. Now, walking has never been my strong point, not since the war when Spike Milligan and I used to lead retreats, and it was also bitterly cold, but walk I did.

I started off in Castlegate, where the most ancient building is the Old Tolbooth, dating from 1627, originally the City's gaol and scene of public executions until 1857. It still preserves the 'Maiden', the sixteenth-century beheading machine said to be the model for the French guillotine.

The Old Tolbooth in Castlegate. It dates from 1627 and was originally the city's gaol and scene of public executions until 1857.

A pleasanter reminder of the past is the Mercat Cross, built in 1686, which is the finest burgh cross in Scotland. A white marble unicorn surmounts the pillar which rises from the centre of this intricately-carved, circular arcade, where licensed meatsellers displayed and sold their products in the market place.

In Broad Street I climbed a flight of steps to visit the

oldest domestic dwelling in the centre of Aberdeen, Provost Skene's House, which is furnished as a period museum. The earliest mention of this building is in 1545 — when Mary Queen of Scots was a little girl of three. Across the street my gaze was caught and held by the astonishing granite façade of Marischal College. It was founded in 1593, but the buildings mostly date from 1837-1844. In 1860 the Marischal and King's Colleges were merged to form the University of Aberdeen.

My only regret about Aberdeen was that I didn't have time to visit the old part of the city — 'Aulton' as the locals call it, a conservation area containing a mixture of dwellings of every century from the sixteenth to the twentieth, all retaining a unity of character and preserving a village atmosphere.

Provost Skene's House. Dating from 1545, it is the oldest surviving domestic building in the city. It has been converted into a museum and shows what life was like for the prosperous citizen through the ages.

Marischal College in Broad Street. One of the largest granite buildings in Europe, it was founded in 1593 as a Protestant rival to the university of King's College. Eventually the two colleges settled their differences and amalgamated to form Aberdeen University.

Below

Wright's and Cooper's Place in Old Aberdeen, which is known locally as 'Aulton'. In the foreground is a decorative metal-sculptured sun-dial.

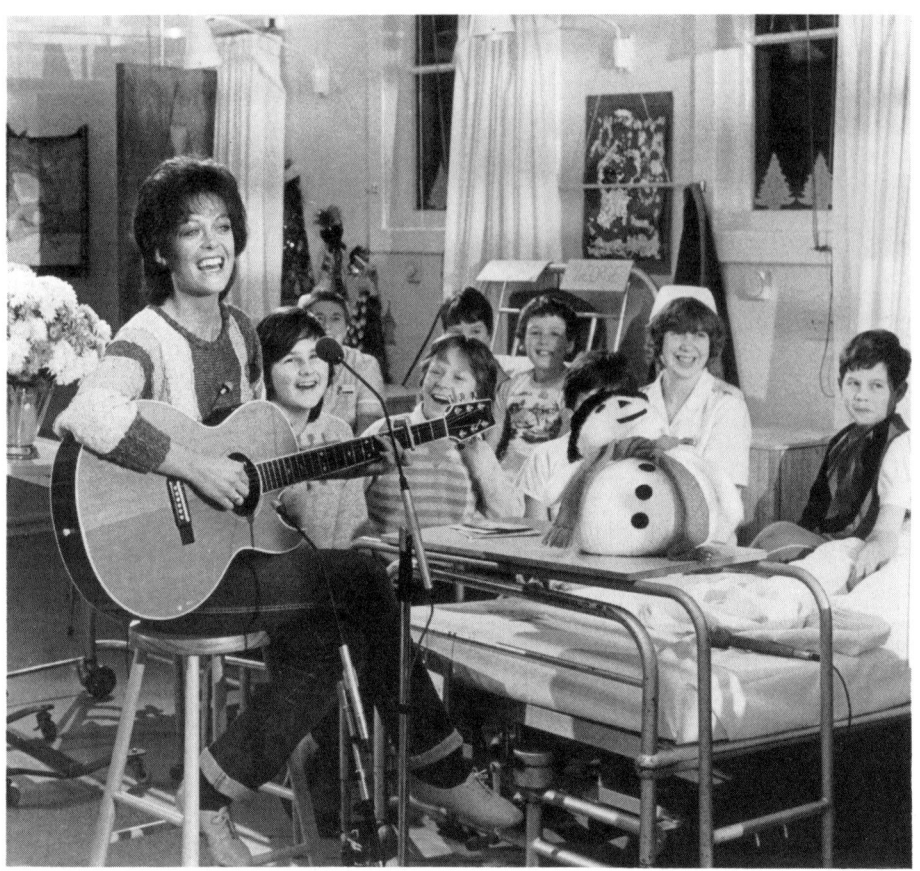

Isla St Clair entertaining the children at the Royal Infirmary. She also accompanied me to Forties Charlie. A bubbling, lively personality, she's great fun to be with.

The following day I returned to the Royal Infirmary and, with Isla St Clair, spent a lot of time in the children's ward. Christmas was very near, the worst time for children to be in hospital. I hope we managed to cheer them up a little.

I had one more major item to perform for the programme. After the rigours of the oil-platform I firmly believed that I was equal to anything that Aberdeen might throw at me. I was wrong. We were filming at night, down in the docks where, accompanied by the Grampian Police Pipe Band, I was going to perform that well-known song, 'Amazing Grace'. It sounded straightforward enough, but it entailed standing around for almost two hours, and I don't remember ever being quite so cold in my entire life!

Yet as I gazed out to the sea, my thoughts turned to those men 110 miles out on Forties Charlie, and to all those other oil-rigs and platforms in the North Sea where men were working in inhospitable conditions in their quest for the black gold under the sea-bed. Compared with them, cut off in the lonely outposts, my temporary discomfort was nothing. I counted my blessings.

Fishing is still an important industry in Aberdeen. But you need to be up early if you want to enjoy the atmosphere of the Fish Market — it opens at 4.30 am. If you want an early kipper you musn't be a late kipper! (It's jokes like this that killed the Variety theatre!)

GLASGOW

Now, I'm going to let you into a secret. My second name is Donald. That's right, I am Harry *Donald* Secombe, and the reason why the 'Donald' came into being is because my father had the idea that somewhere back in the family history we Secombes had Scottish forebears. Despite exhaustive research by my daughter, however, no trace can be found of any such distant connections with Scotland. However, when I was a young lad one of my fondest dreams was of myself wandering through the heather in a Secombe tartan kilt. I imagined fighting valiant battles at the side of Bonny Prince Charlie, cutting swathes through the red-coated English soldiers. There was even a time when I affected a Scottish accent, which went almost unnoticed within the family circle — my father merely thought I had catarrh. And so, albeit mistakenly, I have always regarded Scotland as a kind of second home. I was stationed in various parts of it during the war and sailed from Gourock on the invasion of North Africa in 1942. And I went to war again in Glasgow when I played the Empire there in 1951.

Thus, when 'Highway' was scheduled to visit Glasgow, I was aware of feeling mixed emotions. Scotland I loved; Glasgow I was a bit scared of because of my recollections of the city revolved around my old battle-ground, the Glasgow Empire. The old theatre has gone now but it lives on like a nightmare in the memories of a host of Variety artists who knew and dreaded its fearsome reputation as 'the graveyard of English comics'. There is a saying which originated about the Glasgow Empire that has since been applied to certain clubs 'up North'; 'If they like you, they let you live'. Well, at least they had let me live, though even now, so many years on, my stomach still churned with nervousness at the thought of performing in Glasgow again.

It was Michael Kelly, the Lord Provost, who told me about the 'Glasgow's Miles Better' campaign, which has done a lot to rid the city of the depressing and unfriendly image some people have of it.

143

George Square, the very heart of Glasgow. On the right is the magnificent Victorian City Chambers building.

My first stop was in George Square, at the magnificent City Chambers, an imposing late Victorian edifice in the Renaissance style which was used as the location for the British Embassy in Moscow in Alan Bennett's award-winning television play, 'An Englishman Abroad', starring Coral Browne and Alan Bates. It was here that I met and talked to the Lord Provost of Glasgow, Michael Kelly. The Lord Provost is the equivalent in many ways of the Lord Mayor of London, but whereas the latter is elected for one year, the former's term of office lasts for four years, which means that he has more influence in the long-term running of Scotland's largest city. Michael Kelly told me about the 'Glasgow's Miles Better' campaign, which was recently initiated to rid the city of the depressing and unfriendly image which some people have of it. I do not know how such misconceptions arise, but I can personally vouch for the fact that Glasgow is neither depressing nor unfriendly. The very name of the city has its origins in the Celtic words for 'dear green place', and I was to hear at length about its seventy public parks which offer relaxation and recreational facilities, and its many excellent museums and art galleries, including the world-renowned Burrell Collection.

No one is more conscious of Glasgow's image than Michael Kelly, who believes that its grim and cheerless reputation belongs fifty years ago, certainly not today when, as he said, 'We've got new parks, a new motorway system, pedestrianized precincts, we're on the edge of the best scenery in Scotland — Loch Lomond is only thirty-five minutes' drive from this office — and we want to tell people of the great improvements which are taking place in this city.' Certainly the campaign being pursued with such vigour and enthusiasm by its very young Lord Provost seemed to be achieving its aims.

'Let Glasgow flourish by the preaching of Thy word and the praising of Thy name' is the ancient motto of

Michael Kelly, the Lord Provost. A live-wire if ever there was one, and a great worker for his city.

Cantor Ernest Levy, a most remarkable and inspiring man.

Opposite
The Jewish Choral Choir who sang for the programme in the City Chambers.

the city, and, still in the City Chambers, I was to hear the praises of the Almighty sung in Hebrew by the Jewish Choral Choir. Standing on the steps of the superb marble staircase, they sang 'Kail Dat'. Afterwards I met Cantor Ernest Levy. It was very hard to draw him out on the subject, but in talks I had with him before, during and after the programme, I was able to find out that during the war he had been in no fewer than ten concentration camps, and that on one horrific occasion he had lain for many hours in a mass grave.

What I found so inspiring about Cantor Levy was that not only had he survived all the evil that had been done to him, but that he had emerged from so much suffering without a trace of bitterness. Let him speak for himself: 'Most of us who survived came out mentally and physically destroyed. Some of us managed, with our deep-seated faith, and deep-seated faith in humanity, to work ourselves back into civilization, and into the world, so to speak.'

'What sustained you through those terrible years?' I asked him.

'A very difficult question to answer,' he replied. 'Maybe the inner resources, the ground you got from your parents when you were young; and you don't change fundamentally no matter how hard the times you are in. You try to remain a human being all the time through, and you don't store up your bitterness.'

Instead of a life full of bitterness and regrets, Cantor Levy lives each day joyfully as a bounty granted by God and happily goes about his work as a Cantor and teacher, spending what spare time he has in charitable works, visiting the sick and bringing comfort to many more than his parishoners. At Giffnock and Newlands Synagogue he provides a musical treat every Sabbath and Holy Day for his congregation and those visitors from other synagogues who crowd in to hear him.

I left the City Chambers and walked around. I didn't feel as though I had been brainwashed by Michael Kelly, but I found I was looking at Glasgow through new eyes. Suddenly — and for the first time — I

A traditional Scottish scene — pipers in Buchanan Street.

noticed the width of the main shopping streets, the number of cleaned-up buildings, the general cheeriness of the thronging shoppers. The rest of the day was my own, so I became a tourist, and being a compulsive shopper to boot, Glasgow was just my cup of tea. I walked up and down Argyle Street, Buchanan Street, and the one whose name is known to the world over, whilst remaining almost impossible to spell: Sauchiehall Street. I was slightly puzzled by the number of foreign languages I kept hearing until I remembered reading that Glasgow is an extremely popular place for shopping expeditions from Scandinavia, Iceland and Northern Europe.

Surprisingly, I still hadn't bought anything after traversing the three streets. I was probably saving myself, knowing I was going to end up in the famous 'Barras' market in the city's east end. It differs from Swansea in that it is in the open air, but like all markets it leaves you with the profound conviction that you have come away with a bargain. I was quite convinced as I clutched my guaranteed non-stick saucepans and wended my way back to the hotel.

The next day I had little to do, since Anne Lorne Gilles and Peter Morrison were recording their contribution to the programme, and the weather, as if conspiring with the Lord Provost, turned up trumps by providing a day of rare winter sunshine, the sort that brings colour to your cheeks. It was an opportunity not to be missed. I would see as much of the magnificent scenery around Glasgow as possible in one day.

Now, one of the joys of my job is that it gives me the chance to travel, usually at someone else's expense! I've been luckier than most: I visit Australia at least twice a year, and of course when *Pickwick* was playing on Broadway and then doing a country-wide tour, I saw most of America. Add Hong Kong, Africa and most of the rest of the world, and you'll agree I haven't done too badly. The lesson I've learned in all these places, where visiting time is limited, is this: Don't go off sight-seeing on your own, you're bound to waste time and miss something vital. Don't be blasé, find a local guide, whether a friend or a professional, and you'll be glad you did. Luckily I had a friend in Glasgow who was

only too pleased to show off the beautiful countryside around his city. We visited Loch Lomond, whose banks were no less bonny for being snow-covered, with Ben Lomond towering majestically in the background. We motored on through the glorious Trossachs scenery, and I recalled, on a previous visit to Glasgow, a trip down the Clyde in the *Waverley*, last sea-going paddle steamer in the world. Sadly, I was unable to make the trip this time since the *Waverley* only runs in the summer. I regretted, too, not having enough time to visit Robert Burns country, and pay my respects to Scotland's national poet.

The next morning was back to work time, starting with a drive from the hotel through the city. Glasgow is a lasting tribute to Victorian architects and craftsmen, and yet twentieth-century planners have succeeded in integrating a modern centre which blends smoothly with the architectural heritage of an earlier era. Commenting on the smooth-flowing traffic, I said, 'In London you'd have to travel by underground to move at this speed'.

'Aye', the driver agreed laconically, then added information which surprised me. Glasgow also boasts a very modern subway system. Taking my ignorance and

Opposite top
The beautiful scenery of Loch Lomond is just twenty-odd miles from the city. I visited there — taking the low road of course!

Opposite bottom
The *Waverley* — the last sea-going paddle steamer in the world.

Glasgow is famous for its beautiful parkland. Kelvingrove park is one of many in the city.

surprise to be a slur on his beloved city, the driver became slightly agressive.

'What do you know about its parks?' he demanded.

'Oh, I know about Hampden, Ibrox and Celtic Park', I boasted.

'I'm not talking about footba', he said scathingly. 'I'm talking about Kelvingrove Park, Rouken Glen in Thornliebank, the Kibble Palace, Botanic Gardens . . . '.

The list seemed endless. Only our arrival at our destination, Glasgow Cathedral, saved me from a deluge of information about the glories of Glasgow. Clearly here was one Glaswegian simply bursting with civic pride.

Glasgow really is a city of surprises. This was my tenth 'Highway' programme, and I had thought I was now beyond being stunned by cathedral architecture. And yet here I stood, once more awed and over-whelmed by a cathedral. Standing on a hillside, the building is a fine example of pre-Reformation Gothic architecture, with a tower and spire from the centre. The oldest parts date from the twelfth century, but most of it belongs to the three following centuries. Its crypt, or lower church, is one of the most perfect in Britain. It was built on the site of a monastery founded about 560 by St Mungo, the patron saint of Glasgow, on the banks of a small stream flowing into the Clyde.

The cathedral is as impressively vast inside as Durham Cathedral, yet its beauty is not overshadowed by its vastness. I stood by the tomb of St Mungo and chatted there to that fine Scottish actor, Fulton Mackay, he of the elastic jaw, the brilliant portrayer of the prison warder in the television series 'Porridge', who is invariably outwitted by the incorrigible Fletcher, played by Ronnie Barker. Now, in this perfect setting, he read from the Book of the Prophet Isaiah, Chapter 35:

> *Strengthen ye the weak hands, and confirm the feeble knees.*
> *Say to them that are of a fearful heart, Be strong, fear not: behold, your God will come with vengeance, even God with a recompense; he will come and save you.*

Glasgow Cathedral. A magnificent building, the oldest parts date from the twelfth century. It is dedicated to Glasgow's patron saint and founder, St Mungo.

Then the eyes of the blind shall be opened, and the ears of the deaf shall be unstopped.

Then shall the lame man leap as an hart, and the tongue of the dumb sing: for in the wilderness shall waters break out, and streams in the desert.

And the parched ground shall become a pool, and the thirsty land springs of water: in the habitation of dragons, where each lay, shall be grass with reeds and rushes.

And an highway shall be there, and a way, and it shall be called the way of holiness; the unclean shall not pass over it; but it shall be for those: the wayfaring men, though fools, shall not err therein.

No lion shall be there, nor any ravenous beast shall go up thereon, it shall not be found there; but the redeemed shall walk there.

And the ransomed of the Lord shall return, and come to Zion with songs and everlasting joy upon their heads; they shall obtain joy and gladness, and sorrow and sighing shall flee away.

I was taken back to my hotel by the same driver who had brought me to the Cathedral. He seemed in less chauvinistic mood, but was evidently delighted

Opposite
The actor Fulton Mackay reading from the Book of the Prophet Isaiah inside the Cathedral.

The University. Built in the Gothic style of the fourteenth century, its main feature is the very high tower.

Portrait of the Victorian architect, Sir George Gilbert Scott, who is responsible for the design of the University.

when I suggested that he take me on a tour of his city and show me some of its features. Among the many he pointed out were the University buildings in the west end, erected after the designs of the Victorian architect, Sir George Gilbert Scott in the Gothic style of the fourteenth century, and featuring a high tower. I was reeling with impressions and information by the time I was delivered to my hotel. As I walked from the car, the driver hurled his last and deadliest shaft, stored up for a parting shot:

'And we'll beat you again at the Arms Park next year!'

He was right about that, too.

The next day, I was to sing one of my favourite songs, 'If I can help somebody', down by the dockside, and then record the last words for the programme. It had been an enjoyable few days, and in addition to the now familiar twinge of sadness that I had again only scratched the surface of a place which deserved more intimate acquaintance, my only regret was the fact that an anticipated game of golf at Gleneagles had to be called off because the course lay under several inches of snow. But again, in view of my form in the next game of golf I played in Downpatrick, that was probably a blessing — if not for me, then certainly for any members of the Club who might have been playing on that particular day.

The world-famous Gleneagles golf course. It was closed by a snowfall when I was up there — that snow must have saved me half a dozen golf balls!

Pondering the nature of the Glaswegian character, I posed this question to a famous son of Glasgow, a man whose indomitable spirit has caught the imagination of the country and made him justly renowed:

'How do you define a Glaswegian?'

He replied, 'Glaswegians are tremendously resilient. Here we are in the middle of a depression and I go around Britain and am aware in other major industrial cities of an air of defeatism. People seem beaten. In Glasgow there's an air of vitality and confidence, generated by an attitude that's developed over the years here'. Quoting Sir Harry Lauder's song, 'I belong to Glasgow', he pointed out that it also says 'Glasgow belongs to me'. 'There's no great virtue in being on your knees', he said finally, 'unless it's in prayer to the Supreme Being'.

That is how Jimmy Reid summed up Glasgow for me. One thing is for certain. Glasgow is not on its knees. It's a big, bustling, optimistic place where folk know that the best is yet to be, a city which has lived through depressions in the past and survived them, as it will survive its problems of today, thanks to the resilience of character that Jimmy Reid talked about.

Twelfth-century stained glass panel showing the Prophet Jeremiah, which is held at the world-renowned Burrell Collection.

Photographic Credits

The photographs that appear in this book are the copyright of the following: David Secombe (pages 12, 13, 14, 15, 19, 20, *top and bottom*, 21, 22, 23, 26, 27, 28, 30, 31, 35, 36, 37, 38, 39, 40, 42, 45, 46, 47, 50, 53, 54, 61, 64, *bottom*, 66, *bottom*, 70, 71, 74, 76, *top*, 79, 80, 84, 87, *top*, 88, 90, 92, 93, 95, 99, *top and bottom*, 100, 104, 110 and 111; King's Lynn Museums (page 10); Central Library, King's Lynn (pages 16 and 24); Anglia Television (pages 17, 18, 43, 49 and 55); The Theatre Royal, Bath (page 25); HTV West (pages 32 and 89); Cambridge University Press (page 44); City Engineers Department, Newcastle upon Tyne (pages 58 and 67); The British Tourist Authority (page 60); Tyne & Wear Council (page 62); Newcastle upon Tyne Council (page 63); Tyne Tees Television (pages 66, *top*, 77 and 82); Dean and Chapter Library, Durham (pages 72 and 76); City of Bristol Museum and Art Gallery (page 85); The Tate Gallery, London (page 86); The Theatre Royal , Bristol (page 87); Bristol City Council (page 94); Swansea City Council (pages 102 and 108); HTV Wales (pages 106, 109 and 112); The Northern Ireland Tourist Board (pages 115, *top and bottom*, 120, 122, *top and bottom*, 123, 124 and 125); Ulster Television (pages 116, 118, 126, *top and bottom*); The Ulster Folk and Transport Museum, Cultra (pages 117 and 121); British Petroleum Company Ltd (page 128); Aberdeen Art Gallery and Museums (pages 130 and 131); Aberdeen Tourist Board (pages 132, 134, 135, 138, 139, *top and bottom*, and 141); Grampian Television (page 140); Scottish Tourist Board (pages 37, 150, *top*, and 157); Glasgow District Council (pages 144, 145, 148, 152 and 155); Lewis Segal (page 146); Scottish Television (pages 147 and 154); The Waverley Steam Navigation Company (page 150, *bottom*); Mr K.J. Fraser, FILAM, Dip LD, Director of Parks and Recreation (page 151); The Royal Institute of British Architects (page 156); Glasgow Museums and Art Galleries, The Burrell Collection (page 159).